RISING TECHNOMASS

THE POLITICAL ECONOMY OF SOCIAL TRANSFORMATION IN CYBERSPACE

Jose Fuentes
Satyananda Gabriel

published by Jonkonnu Press,
an imprint of Westry Wingate Group, inc.,
2708 Wet Stone Way, Suite 108
Charlotte, North Carolina, USA 28208

Westry Wingate Group, Inc.
http://www.westrybooks.com

1. technology 2. economics 3. internet
4. sociology 5. politics

ISBN-13 978-1-935323-02-0
ISBN-10 1-935323-02-4

printed in the United States of America

the publisher, by agreement with the authors, will donate 10% of the net proceeds from this text to the following: the Mediawiki Foundation (5%) and the Creative Commons Foundation (5%)

the authors thank Ella Gabriel for her indispensable editing and InDesign expertise without which this text would never have seen the light of day.

RISING TECHNOMASS

THE POLITICAL ECONOMY OF SOCIAL TRANSFORMATION IN CYBERSPACE

Jose Fuentes
Satyananda Gabriel

In our analysis, focusing on economic development, a relevant view would be that culture serves in a basic function to store knowledge. Over time man accumulates, advances and transforms his useful knowledge which is really stored by culture. As man interacts with culture and applies the knowledge stored by culture he originates new forms of technology.... Technology cannot, to our view, be correctly conceptualized and analyzed outside the culture matrix.

— Richard L. Brinkman,
Cultural Economics (1981)

To my parents,
Roberto Fuentes and Marlene Aguilar De Fuentes.
And to Mary McCrady

—Jose Fuentes

For Chelvanaya

—Satyananda Gabriel

0

Preface

The style of this text, a collaboration between an economist (former computer programmer, corporate executive, and sometime poet, among other vocations) and a visual artist with a background in psychology, film, and computer science (currently a research fellow at Carnegie Mellon), is not surprisingly out of the usual textual box. It is simultaneously a work of theory, visual art, and prose-poetry. It is meant to reflect (as a two-way mirror) both the out-of-control-ness of Cyberspace (where open has taken on multiple meanings) and the ongoing struggle to redefine humanity by shaping new types of social relationships, new understandings of individuality, and new possibilities for human creativity and communication.

The struggle continues ....

"The empires of the future are the empires of the mind."

—Winston Churchill

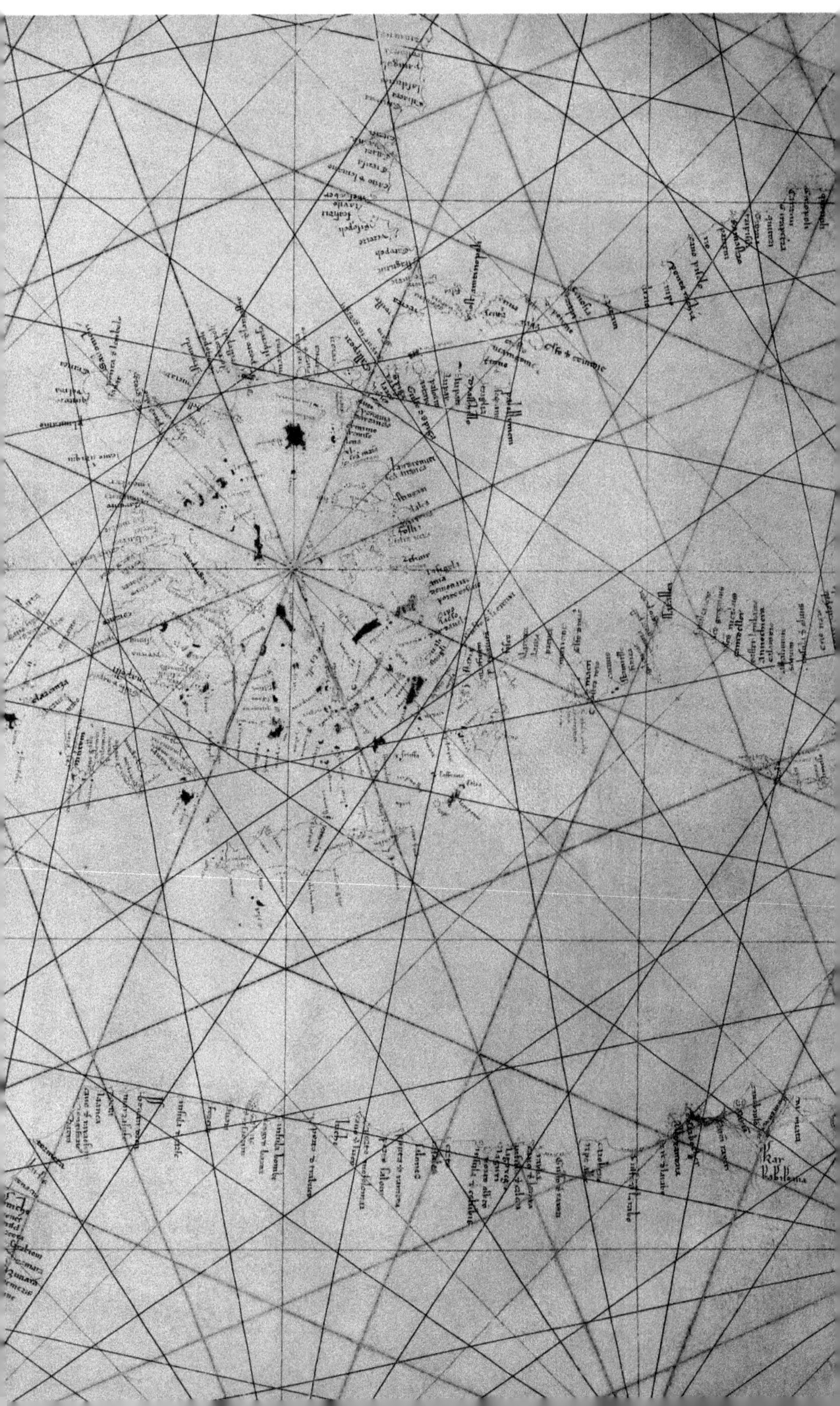

########
we begin:

1

Jack Amariglio and David Ruccio penned an article titled "From Unity to Dispersion: The Body in Modern Economic Discourse," that was featured in the text, Postmodernism, Economics, and Knowledge (2001) that reminded us of the contingent nature of the human being and the fact that economic theory had long placed the human being at the center of discourse. The rise of neoclassical economics marked the end of self-consciousness in economic discourse, with human agency reduced to a simple algorithm and the social constitution of humanness removed from consideration altogether. The concept of humanity rigidified within the neoclassical framework and then slipped out of the debate altogether, leaving most mainstream economists without the ability to recognize, much less challenge, either the humanist presumptions of their theoretical framework or the dangers of conceiving human beings as behavioral simpletons. What remained was homo economicus, a Benthamite robot, a caricature of what it is to be human, and disconnected from the larger cultural context within which real human agents live or the institutional framework whose rules shape human decision sets and perception in the context of such cultural influences.

In the real world, as opposed to the world of mainstream economic thinking, human beings are shaped by a complex interaction of cultures and genetics. We can do very bizarre and irrational things, sometimes (often) en masse. Witch hunts and inquisitions, mass panics, human sacrifice, celebratory lynchings of socially constructed Others (once a tradition in the United States), investment manias, fads, and any number of other instances of masses under the influence of transient cultural norms are not illusions or insignificant deviations from an otherwise rational human existence but important and persistent aspects of human society. One can certainly hope that, over time, humans may evolve to be more rational or, at least, less prone to instances of mass insanity, but it is not prudent to base one's social scientific analysis on hopes or social scientific fictions (as is too often the case with mainstream economic theory).

Herd behavior, uncritical acceptance of and conformity to cultural mores, adaptation to institutional rules and structures, even when those rules and structures lead to negative impacts on individuals or the society at large, including the adapting individual, and large scale cultural transformations that alter behavioral norms, often the result of technological innovation, environmental changes, or social events is common in human society and call into question models of society or decision making that presume stasis in these cultural norms. Equilibria in social processes are always temporary and contingent at best and often completely non-existent. Humans are social beings, shaped by social demands and constraints and, at times, compelled by irrational but persistent beliefs to surges of violence, even genocide. Although multiculturalism has received a great deal of attention in countries as diverse as the United States and Canada, France, China, Malaysia, and Brazil, the conditions for abandoning the idea of the alien and often hated Other and for abandoning racist points of view (since the concept of race is based on a genetic fiction) are quite clearly not yet present. Explicit racist language has given way to euphemisms and proxy issues that, because of racism, can be blown out of all reasonable proportion (such as the movement to label President Obama as an illegitimate president because he is "not a native-born American," despite clear evidence that he was born in Hawaii, while his 2008 opponent was given a free pass on this issue despite being ambiguously native-born, having been born in the Panama Canal Zone) but the impact of racist points of view continues to severely limit opportunities for a subset of people, results in their being routinely stereotyped, and at the same time privileging another subset. And sometimes racism leads to violence and even murder. This behavior may not be rational but it is, unfortunately, all too human. In other words, there are times it would be nice if the neoclassical fantasies of cultural homogeneity, rationality, and super humanness was true.

Mainstream economists also like to talk about the rationality of decision making when viewed in the long term. Humans are perceived not only as extraordinary processors of data in the short term but as capable of incorporating future outcomes in their decision calculus. Again, it would be nice if true, but the reality of human life is something altogether different. What we humans don't know is vast, while what we do know is miniscule, by comparison, despite our collective and individual hubris. And, in some larger sense, even the most rational behaviors may turn out to be irrational in the long run. Rapid economic growth that results in a concomitant alteration in environmental conditions (air and water, even the chemical composition of human bodies), such as we have witnessed in various locales and are currently witnessing in China, for example, appears quite rational in a current income sense (who doesn't want to be richer in material things?), but as humanity stumbles towards an environmental catastrophe the short-run economic gains may eventually pale before longer term damage to human survival. To think that we know the answer to this question, while proceeding merrily on our way down the current path, may turn out to be the ultimate case of hubris.

We can never be entirely sure that human decisions, including those taken by large groups conforming to mass culture or just following orders from a centralized authority, are the best or optimal or even sensible decisions. Human society is still in a process of evolution and we can't even be sure we're evolving along the best possible path. We can just be sure that we are and always will be in a state of change. We are social beings, taught various ways of perceiving ourselves, others, and the world we inhabit, lacking omniscience, not always or even predominantly rational, subject to continual surprises, even at our own decisions and the consequences of those decisions, and prone to all sorts of unfounded biases. We learn from our parents and others, even when what we learn, such as beliefs in magical/mystical properties for skin pigmentation or other phenotypical characteristics, have absolutely no basis in reality. We copy each other, giving into peer pressure. Some of us have even been known to do the most idiotic stunts because of peer pressure and/or mimicry, such as "surfing" atop moving cars or elevators, "planking" on escalators, or consuming alcohol through eyeballs. Rational? Be serious.

Another enormous hole in mainstream economic theory is the failure to address political power, the exercise of it, influence over it, and the shaping of it. Political power is an important determinant not only of market processes, but also of culture and all those human decisions formed by cultural understanding (or misunderstanding). Political power, culture, economics, technology, and the natural environment are always interacting and reshaping each other and the human agents who are the subject of social scientific theory, including economic theories (mainstream and otherwise).

These forces came together to create the Internet and to shape the the way in which the Internet has evolved. But the evolutionary path of the Internet was not determined solely by centralized authorities, political, economic, or cultural. It has been shaped by the actions and ideas of countless individuals and a large number of institutions, some of which have little in common except an interest in the future of this new technological invention and/or its effects. It takes an extraordinary naivete to believe that the decisions shaping the path to Cyberspace were not the result of a complex interplay of sometimes contradictory political, cultural, economic, and environmental processes or of struggles to secure the conditions for the reproduction of a status quo that would eventually be problematized by these same technologies. The Internet was not predetermined, but the result of the very determinate configurations of these struggles during its formative period and ever since. It is not an exaggeration or hyperbole to say that the continued struggle over the rules that will bound (constrain) Cyberspace has implications for the future of human evolution.

Ironically, the decentralized, anti-authoritarian bent to the Internet was, to a significant extent, the result of the U.S. military's role in the development of the technologies. Through the Defense Advanced Research Projects Agency (DARPA), one of the most centralized institutional structures in the world, the U.S. military, shepharded the development of an almost anarchic institutional structure to meet the objective of developing such intricate redundancies of alternative and relatively autonomous nodes for flows of digital information that even a nuclear attack would not likely obliterate the functioning of the Internet, as a repository for critical information necessary for reproducing the basic institutions, contracts, and financial data underpinning existing power and wealth configurations in American society, particularly the corporate structures that dominate social (and not just work) life and are critical to existing distributions of power and wealth within American society. Indeed, the very basis for the political and cultural foundations that generate social norms and rules is information. The recognition that digitized information is easier to replicate, store, and diffuse (making it less vulnerable than physical documents) led to the creation of the Internet as a relatively autonomous space for digital information flow and providing the basis for the evolution of Cyberspace, a world where digitized information has become the substance for new forms of communication, new relationships, and new types of economic and social interchange, including some forms of interchange that have posed a challenge to at least a subset of corporate structures and governments.

The concept of technomass, a superorganic body,

comprised of countless individual human actors who are constituted, in part, by their participation in this superorganic body called Cyberspace, is one of the unintended consequences of creating such an autonomous, decentralized space. The paradigm of corporate dominance over social, including but not limited to commercial and productive, life is under challenge within this new body. And make no mistake, the technomass is a new living entity that acts both collectively and through individual members, operating according to a sharing paradigm that is most often at odds with the old corporate paradigm. Where corporate structures want to use the state as a vehicle to enforce their private property rights and provide the infrastructure for commoditizing both products and ideas, the technomass seeks to transfer rights related to a large subset of digitized data and code to the collective sphere and then to diffuse access and control to the public (or at least that subset who are members of the technomass). Thus, the technomass alters economic life and undermines the conditions of reproduction of some corporate entities, even while creating new commercial and productive spaces for other corporate entities, as well as for autonomously acting individual human agents. In a larger sense, the technomass interacts with the conditions of existence of capitalism, an economic system predicated on the lack of autonomy of the vast majority of corporate employees. Access to digital information and the ability to forge relationships around exchange of such information, sometimes while working within existing corporate structures subject to now weakened constraints on behavior (at least for "white collar" workers), challenges existing conditions of existence of corporate capitalism, at least in its previous incarnations.

The technomass is understood as rising because it is increasing, in size and reach, in every moment. In addition to its impact upon the dominant economic system, the rising technomass constitutes one of the forces reshaping what it is to be a human being, reconstituting the nature of the human body/being. The synthesis of human thought and information technologies, the way Cyberspace has become a nexus for human relationships and a wide range of exchanges, and the transformations in thinking and decision sets generated by participation in the technomass alter the decision making processes of human subjects, producing new and unpredictable outcomes for social processes that are also being transformed.

The rising technomass is manifested most intimately in the proliferating communities of code sharers, sometimes referred to as hackers, who occupy Cyberspace as renegades and organizers. The technomass provides both the means to resist commodification of code and to simultaneously provide some firms with the means to valorize their commodities. This valorization takes place when a firm links its commodities to code generated within the technomass, such as simple algorithms packaged as applications that may be attached to existing products, enhancing such products in ways that add value without the firm selling the product having to pay for this added value. Firms that can tap into the technomass in this way are likely to gain competitive advantages over those unable to do so and firms that go so far as to oppose the technomass, perhaps by challenging the right of hackers to distribute and share code are likely to find themselves increasingly at odds with the very community they need to survive.

In order to understand the implications of the rising technomass, it is necessary for social theory to problematize the linkages between firms and humans, both within and outside of the technomass, both of which are in flux, changed by the very dynamics of Cyberspace and the rising technomass within Cyberspace. Social theory simultaneously needs to problematize the nature of the human body/being, to recognize that human subjectivity is a variable, not a constant, and is being altered by participation in Cyberspace.

In a sense, humanity and the individual human being are just as much a manifestation of technology (where increasingly organic is fused with non-organic) as of nature and, in this sense, the human being may be viewed as simply a more complex form of machinery. Certainly this reality is not lost on some corporate managers and directors who explore ways to extend intellectual property rights to the machinery and code (DNA) of individual human bodies. The intersection of humanism and corporatism become glaring in the legal/political debate over the often contradictory rights of individual homo sapiens and corporations. This debate has largely decoupled intellectual property rights (IPR) from the notion of invention, which was supposedly the foundation for IPR. When the code being debated is DNA, it is difficult to argue that the code was invented by corporate actors.

It is ironic that a theoretical framework as grounded in utopian humanism as neoclassical economics would ultimately serve as instrument for defending and extending corporate power at the expense of individual human beings, but such is clearly the case. Thus, the technomass, and especially that subset of the technomass called hackers, is fundamentally at odds with the neoclassical way of thinking, even as it shares a suspicion of authoritarian power. The problem is that the neoclassical framework fails to recognize all forms of authoritarian power except that weilded by governments, while the technomass recognizes the synthesis of government and corporate power, seeing the former as frequently conspiring with the latter to deny rights to code sharing and code proliferation in order to protect often arbitrarily restrictive notions of IPR that allow the corporate structures to both valorize product and to deny the possibility of inventions that are outside of the control of corporate structures.

This text recognizes the problematic nature of this struggle between real human beings and bureaucratic, centralized, authoritarian institutions with wide ranging powers in the society. It also recoznizes the similarly bureaucratic, centralized, and authoritarian nature of the economics profession, specifically, and academia, more generally, in conspiring with corporate structures to advance theories that simultaneously treat human beings as transcendental, homo economicus, rather than recognizing them as changing organisms whose identity is constantly made problematic by interventions from a wide range of sources, including governments, corporations, the natural environment, and other human beings. Humans exist in struggle, not in equilibria. Humans exist as a component part of a larger techno-social-environmental gestalt that is, itself, in constant flux and always subject to crises. In this sense, the concept of technomass is deliberately referential to the fusion of human and non-organic technology and to the ability of humans to reorganize into new types of communities from which to intervene in shaping the society of which they are a part.

The technomass is disruptive of old forms of behavior, old institutional relationships, old forms of communication, and countless types of social relationships, including romantic love, organizational management, and parent-child discourse. The technomass is also disruptive of thinking patterns of individual homo sapien sapiens. One does not think the same way in Cyberspace, nor is the change in thinking singular. In recent memory we have seen the near death of the written letter and the explosion in communication by email and instant messaging. Cyberspace will continue to change the way we "talk" to one another, in all our various social roles, whether as workers, managers, husbands, wives, brothers, sisters, sons, and daughters, community activists, or political provocateurs. All these changes represent molecules in a giant wave of social transformation, a society in flux. Every aspect of relationships and thinking are undergoing radical transformations and the process of change is constant and global. The consequences of these changes are also constant and global, therefore difficult to pin down at any singular moment. Nevertheless, it should be clear that these changes are critical to the way politics, economics, and culture function. In other words, these changes are constitutive of all those social processes that make up the realm of study of the social sciences. If social scientists do not adapt to this environment of radical transformation, they will fail to function optimally as interpreters of social reality, engineers of more efficient organizational strategies, or any of their typical goals and objectives.

This text is, in part, meant to challenge all of us, including the social scientists, to move beyond the conservative philosophical foundations that make it difficult for them to recognize and adapt to these changes. If we are to understand economic change, and the forces that drive humanity in one direction versus another (for example, towards producing more value versus less, towards generating global climate changes that may threaten human existence versus some more benign climatological outcome, to more versus less violent conflicts, towards famines versus a world where no human child must go without sufficient nutrition to survive, much less thrive), then we must learn to adapt our theoretical frameworks to a world that is far more complex and changeable than is recognized in our currently dominant paradigms. Perhaps social scientists might learn new ways of collaborating and innovating from the technomass, where change is an important part of the moment to moment functioning of code writing and critique, hacking, collaborating, and communicating.

Richard L. Brinkman in his path breaking work, Cultural Economics (1981), proposed a new general theory of economic development grounded in the notion that technology, in the form of both ideas and concrete artifacts (the physical manifestation of our technological innovation), is the substance driving the process of economic growth and development (and, in a larger sense, cultural evolution). In this context, the introduction of the technologies innovated to generate the social space commonly referred to as Cyberspace (from William Gibson's original use in Neuromancer) have dramatically altered the technological foundation for human culture, creating new possibilities heretofore only envisioned in science fiction.

It is our assertion that Cyberspace has brought unprecedented visibility and connectedness to human societies and the individuals who comprise them (a condition for the existence and rise of the technomass). It has allowed for the diffusion of knowledge to every corner of the planet, creating the effect of speeding up the structural transformation in global and local economic structures and relationships. Unfortunately, mainstream economics has little to say on this transformation, being trapped in a culturally narrow-minded, pre-industrial, pre-Freudian model of human behavior (psychology) without any recognition of the impact of technology in shaping both social systems and human psychology. Given the dominance of neoclassical economic theory in shaping public policy, there is a vast void between the reality of technological and structural transformations and the political economy of regulating those transformations.

The problem is that theory is also a form of technology and those who benefit from the existing structure of social relationships have a vested interest in shaping theory(ies) to fit their pragmatic/selfish needs for reproducing such relationships. Thus, it is not only political leaders who have been captured within a network of elite social structures designed to maintain a status quo that may be quite outdated (if it was ever really optimal) and even dangerous to the future of humanity, but the same can be said of intellectual samurai, such as academic economists practicing sophisticated mathematical and statistical techniques in the context of economic assumptions that are obviously at odds with easily obtainable facts.

However, Cyberspace has a potential response to this problem of cultural lag (where social and intellectual structures are resistant to change and primarily serve as tools for reproducing outdated social relationships, while physical technology is changing at an exponential rate) by creating new social structures for production and distribution of value, the sharing of useful information and creative ideas, and the securing and reproduction of social relationships.

The artificial, human constructed boundaries and identities (e.g. race and nationality) that have divided humanity and served as fodder for wars, exploitation, and countless violations of human rights and dignity are far more fragile within Cyberspace. The ability to transcend these boundaries, to circumvent the narrow restrictions of states and other closed clubs, has never been greater. We have learned to interact within Cyberspace, to live there, in ways that trivialize the old boundaries. Our Facebook friends need not be from the old neighborhood. And the "news" informing our understanding of the world and serving as catalyst for social action need not be from the old, established institutions referred to as "the Fourth Estate," but can originate from Cybercitizens/Netizens with their own equipment for capturing and transmitting images and text virtually instantly and pervasively within Cyberspace. The time when governments or other mega-institutions could act in the darkness to subvert human rights and freedoms has become highly problematic. We share freely with one another and we have learned to do so within the intermediaries of the past. Thus, to the extent that such subversions continue, it must be reproduced by blocking the revolutionary effects of Cyberspace, by imposing censorship and political firewalls between people, by denying access to the technologies available for diffusion of knowledge, and/or by artificially raising the cost of such access.

Thus, nothing is guaranteed. These new and potentially liberating technologies may fall under the control of institutional structures that have no interest in building a world where respect for human rights and the diffusion of knowledge are commonplace. It is not difficult to identify uses of Cyberspace that run counter to our more positive vision of this space, whether in the form of organized criminal enterprises using Cyberspace to steal money and identities, the Chinese government's collaboration with certain corporate structures to enforce its control over Cyberspace, or Google's collection of massive amounts of personal information for its own corporate objectives (and sharing this information with other institutional structures, including governments). Such institutional structures may ultimately reshape technologies in ways that reinforce old boundaries, reproduce proprietary control over information, and push humanity further along a path of irrational divisions and ultimate extinction.

Nevertheless, such subversion of the positive potential of Cyberspace (William Gibson's vision was certainly darker) will take some doing because the formation of a complex and ever changing web of interconnected people and technologies outside of traditional spheres of centralized control (the decentralized Technomass) has never been stronger or more "out of control" than it is today. Cyberspace is creating a culture of freedom. We do not want the old boundaries any more because the only purposes they serve are negative, blocks to human progress, tools for the reproduction of obsolete\ possibilities of crossing boundaries and interacting with one another without an intermediary serving as border guard. The sharing of knowledge, open source invention and innovation, has always been a dynamic force in the survival and advance of humanity. Ironically, we may have rediscovered our true human essence within this technologically constructed Cyberspace.

2

It is clear that the information technology revolution has had a positive impact on the ability of corporations to generate cash flow growth, on improving the underlying productivity of workers, and on facilitating more rapid turnover in markets. In other words, like previous technological revolutions, the growth of Cyberspace and related technologies, is having a wide-scale impact on wealth creation. But was this impact apparent from the start of the revolution?

In exploring the relationship between technology and capitalist social relationships, David M. Gordon asked the question "Is it possible for capitalists to deploy technologies and job structures which "control" workers if those elements of production are not "cost-minimizing"?"

This question is particularly interesting because it reflects the consistent, cross-theoretic tendency of economists, whether orthodox (neoclassical) or heterodox (in this case, Marxian) to essentialize efficiency (cost minimization, profit maximization, etc.) and the fact that it is within the Marxian intellectual tradition (at least the economics version represented, in the above instance, by David M. Gordon) where one finds the most consistent *and* coherent narrative addressing the relationship between technological and social transformations. Indeed, other than some institutionalist economists, the Marxian economists have been most likely to recognize that technology is not simply a mechanical equation relating inputs to outputs but simultaneously both a set of cultural artifacts reflecting the "state of the art" in human interventions into nature and a component in the cultural DNA that shapes human behavior, including what neoclassical economists describe as preference orderings.

Many of the mainstream studies on the impact of information technology have focused on this question of efficiency, but have done so from the perspective that technology is simply an equation relating outputs to inputs, rather than something deeper in the DNA of human society. Many of these studies share with orthodox Marxian theory a presumption that information technology would not be implemented within capitalist corporate structures if it was not a driver for increased efficiency, higher rates of exploitation, and higher rates of profit. It is assumed that managers of capitalist corporate structures are "profit maximizing" in their decisions and therefore would never adopt a technology (which is the basis of a particular form of "production function," the aforementioned equation) and that profit maximization implies efficiency. However, the reality is that information technology has been widely adopted within corporate structures without any prior unambiguous indication of an efficiency effect. Capitalism is not the utopian, science fiction, mechanistic social system that rests at the core of both neoclassical economic theory and orthodox Marxian theory. Capitalism is a system based on deploying wage laborers (who have voluntarily contracted a period of their life time to work for a determinant firm) to produce commodities that can be converted into cash, where this cash embodies both the wages of the workers, the cost of the raw materials and other consumed inputs (including both hard and soft technology inputs), and a surplus that becomes the basis for reproducing all those relationships in society necessary to capitalism's continued existence. One element of this last fraction of the value *(surplus value)* created by wage workers in a capitalist system is called profit.

Do managers in capitalist firms opt for new forms of technology because the result of such implementation is higher profit or even lower unit costs (cost minimization)? Or do managers behave like everyone else in society and respond to cultural signals, trends, fads, and prejudices?

Cyberspace, an embodiment of information technology and a portal through which information technology can be transmitted across geographic space and diffused throughout human culture, represents a paradigm shift in a wide array of cultural processes. Involvement in Cyberspace, in part through the adoption of specific technologies within workspaces, has become critical to participation in the larger culture where these technologies have not simply been adopted, but have become catalysts for dramatic changes in culture. In other words, without respect to positive increases in output per person hour of work, rates of exploitation, cost minimization, or any of the typical economic variables (of mainstream or heterodox vintage), new technologies are adopted, to a significant extent, because to not do so would be to make one's workspaces less "sexy," less "modern" and therefore less attractive to employees, customers, managers, directors, owners, and media observers who write the "glossy" pieces that sell the idea of capitalist success (whether or not any objective numbers exist to justify this perception of the successfulness of replicating such cultural norms). Corporate structures adopt some technologies so pervasively that it ceases to be necessary to demonstrate that such technologies are efficient—everyone is using them, so by definition they must be efficient. Once everyone is using them and the alternative is no longer considered appropriate, which may mean that financiers are unwilling to support the adoption of such alternatives, then the standard by which efficiency would be measured is corrupted or completely absent or ignored. Failure to adopt the technologies could very well lead to some instances of greater production efficiency (such as workers who lose less time surfing the web for non work-related reasons or less company resources expended to plug security holes created by the new technologies). The perception that such workspaces are not "modern" and therefore not "competitive" could produce reactions that make perception into reality. The less "modern" company may lose customers or attract less innovative employees and therefore be at a competitive disadvantage.

In other words, Cyberspace is generating a cultural shift by which it gets reproduced and expanded into more and more realms of work and social life without regard to the efficiency outcomes that are so often attributed to capitalism. We want to be in Cyberspace, whether or not we're more productive there. Just as more and more people want to be on Facebook, even at work or when in classrooms "listening" to lectures.

The fact that technological innovation may sometimes (or even often) be driven by cultural, rather than simply economic, criteria does not, however, mean the innovation have not had a dramatic impact on economic processes. Productivity improvements are apparent in the above average growth in free cash flows and related incomes and security valuations. The process of globalization has been, in part, driven by these technological innovations which have dramatically reduced the relevance of geographic distances, allowing production processes to be decentered and scattered about the globe. The process of decentering production and other economic processes has allowed for the exploitation of low cost laborers in poor countries, serving transnational firms headquartered in the core capitalist nations.

The powerful and consistent push to integrate Cyberspace into work life has only added to the growth of the technomass, with millions of individuals able to continue to interface with the larger technomass even at work. This is a boon to the *Open Source Movement*, which represents one of the most prominent manifestations of the technomass and is having a revolutionary impact on innovation within the software sector. Millions of people collaborating on software allows for more creativity and more rapid innovation than might be the case within any individual corporate structure, even giant firms like Microsoft, Apple, and Google. The innovations gifted to the world within the Open Source Movement provide important ideas and digital raw material for countless companies, as well as individuals, crafting new types of computer algorithms to solve problems or provide new technics for interacting within Cyberspace.

Thus, the technomass as an autonomous, self-directed force may ultimately have a bigger impact on social evolution than capitalism, itself. It may even be the precursor to a new economic system, assuming the guardians of the old system are unable to short circuit the wide scale changes by which the new system displaces the old.

THIS IS AN EXPLORATION. AN EXPLORATION OF TRANSFORMATION

THE ONGOING
(NEVER STOPPING)
TECHNOLOGICAL
METAMORPHOSIS
OF THE
STRUCTURES
THAT SHAPE

REALITY NOW

THE NOW IS TODAY, YESTERDAY, AND A TOMORRO#W THAT WILL NEVER TASTE THE SAME AS THE SAME AS THE
PRESENT MOMENT THAT IS D#, FLEETING THAT IT HAS ALREADY BECOME YESTERDAY AS YOU READ

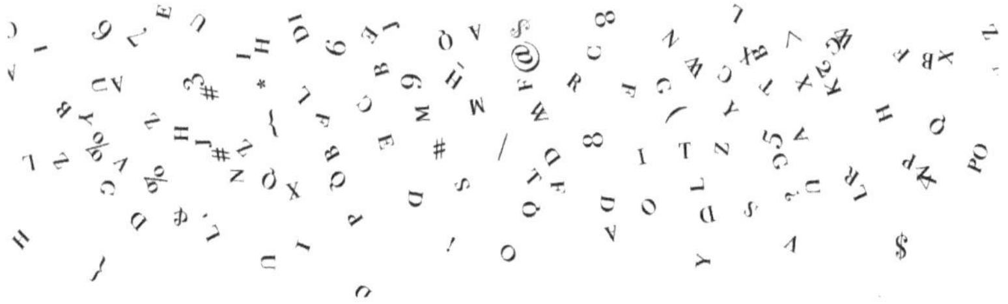

HERACLITUS TAUGHT US,
NOTHING ENDURES BUT CHANGE

YOU ALREADY KNOW THIS,
THIS IS NOT QUITE NEW.

+ THIS IS AS OLD AS THE BIG BANG +

WHY IS THIS RELEVANT?

(DEPENDS ON WHO IS ASKING, OF COURSE)

FOR YOU...

##############O
IO###
#############O#########################IOII##################

...FOLLOW US IF YOU MAY

3

The first relationship of a human being to the creative output of her imagination and hands is a relationship of intimate connection: my *art* is my *self*. *I am what I create*. This relationship between a human and the output of her work was important to many of the early philosophers who attempted to conceptualize what we now call economic relationships, although perhaps no philosopher was more focused upon this issue than Karl Marx, whose work has become implicitly or explicitly taboo precisely because of this.

The primitive act of *taking* from the creative actor the fruits of her creation is the beginning moment of a new society. The process of transforming this taking into normality (in its first moment, it must have been obviously anything but normal) is the process of normalizing the new society based on taking but where taking is no longer perceived, in mainstream culture, as taking. Marx (and Engels, who completed the editing) described this normalization in his three volume work, *Capital*. An important aspect of the normalization of economic takings occurred through a popular focus upon market processes (the realm of "equality"): masking the taking by creating the illusion of voluntary and equal exchange. No place epitomizes the realm of this illusion more than Cyberspace, where equality is embedded in the mythology of these new technologies: Cyberspace, far more than markets, has become *the* metaphor for freedom and equality.

Beyond the realm of freedom and equality was the world of actual production relationships where Marx described the often violent and certainly coercive processes by which taking is the foundation and coercion the fact of everyday life. If workers were not already dispossessed, Marx argued, then how could they be enticed to voluntarily agree to their own exploitation?

Taking and coercion are not apparently present in most market relationships and most interactions within Cyberspace (although it would be a stretch to argue that coercion and taking are completely banished from these spheres).

The primitive accumulation of capital was the original theft of value leading to the creation of new types of society. Kidnapping human beings into slavery, the use of organized violence to coerce people into performing labor services or producing goods for particular *lords*, and dispossession of families from land and other means of production such that the only means for livelihood must be obtained by selling labor-time were all examples of primitive accumulation, which led to social formations where officially sanctioned theft (which Marx called *exploitation*) became a fact of life. These societies are described in the literature as slavery, feudalism, and, more recently, capitalism. The evolution of Cyberspace has taken place in the context of this latter type of society, capitalism. Nevertheless, Cyberspace simultaneously presents an opportunity for fostering capitalist relationships and a potential threat to that same system. Like markets, Cyberspace provides an ideological screen for exploitation: the aforementioned realm of freedom and equality, which becomes the focus of popular imagination and diverts attention from exploitation. On the other hand, Cyberspace represents a very real realm where it becomes possible to escape the bonds of exploitative relationships.

This latter possibility comes from the fact that creative actors within Cyberspace have found new and collective ways to avoid becoming alienated from their creative work. This has occurred through democratically (or anarchistically) sharing code. Writing and revising code among a collective of creative actors is the most revolutionary aspect of Cyberspace from a social standpoint. This is the foundation for the Open Source Movement. The Open Source Movement represents a serious challenge, if not outright threat, to the paragons of capitalist production of code, epitomized by Microsoft. Indeed, the struggle between the large-scale capitalist code producing firms and the anarchistic technomass of open source code sharers and users is often viewed in terms of the struggle between Microsoft and the community of hackers—a conflict that is almost Biblical in the information technology universe.

Cyberspace has created an open environment where masses are forming without the hierarchical (top-down) control mechanisms in place that had been critical to the post primitive accumulation model and subsequent exploitative social structures and formations. These masses act spontaneously to create alliances, to collaborate, to share, to develop new technologies that circumvent attempts at external control over their creative actions within Cyberspace, and to develop their own means for policing, distributing, and organizing resources. Despite being bound together by non-pecuniary motives, these masses are a competitive threat to many existing social institutions, particularly those capitalist corporate structures dependent upon so-called intellectual property rights over digital (or digitizable) creative output.

The independent and anarchic nature of the rising technomasses may represent the most serious challenge to authority structures and to capitalist corporate structures (and the culture upon which these structures are dependent) that has developed during the 21st century, arguably more of an immediate threat to the cash flows of Microsoft than the fundamentalist religious movements that have occasionally spawned "terrorist" attacks upon social formations and the physical artifacts of those social formations. The latter can be more easily understood as criminal acts and addressed as such, including by meeting violence with greater violence. On the other hand, as both Gandhi and Martin Luther King understood, violence can be more easily justified as a response to violence than as a response to peaceful acts of resistance to authority. In other words, even if it was possible to identify the black hat hackers of the world (much less the white hat versions, who may be just as threatening to authorities), it might not be so easy to send predator drones to take them out. The rising technomass is, for the most part, peaceful and, except to a subset of corporate structures, either benign or beneficial (especially to individual users of the new technologies that constitute Cyberspace or small corporate structures developing their business plans around open source software). The small number of dominant American motion picture firms (heretofore referred to as Hollywood) may hate digital "piracy" but there are countless individuals living in places without easy access to Hollywood movies who are now able to download and view them. Is this a bad thing, even for Hollywood? Perhaps the real problem is that Hollywood is controlled by individuals lacking the vision to adapt to the new technologies (rather than attacking them). Ironically, the spread of Hollywood movies around the world may be doing more to "Westernize" populations than any other social or military intervention, which is certainly in the long-term interest of not only Hollywood but the larger community of "Western" capitalist firms and related governments. Just as Cyberspace provides a venue for individuals to cooperate in challenging authoritarian regimes or socially irresponsible corporations, it also provides a space for democratic ideals and notions of human rights to be widely diffused, further stimulating resistance to injustice. In this sense, Cyberspace is a space for fostering revolutions of many kinds.

the institutions that comprise the socio-political-economic sphere — industrial, financial, commercial, household, and centralized bureaucratized governmental

and

the boundaries that separate one from the other, in a world where technological change is increasing at an increasing rate are becoming

increasingly
anachronistic
and widening

cultural

lag muy muy rapido

4

Cyberspace transcends nation-states, yet remains subject to the interventions of specific nation-states. No where is this more obvious and well publicized than in the interventions of the government of the People's Republic of China (PRC). Chinese participants in the rising technomass have come up against a government that is fiercely resisting the anarchistic tendency of that movement and coercing corporate structures that are dependent upon Cyberspace to cooperate in enforcing censorship and breaching privacy. The technomasses act spontaneously to resist these efforts. The most adept elements of the technomass can circumvent the so-called *Great Firewall of China*, but it is clear that the efforts of the PRC regime have, nevertheless, been successful at intimidating the vast majority of Chinese citizens, which has resulted in a large degree of self-censorship. Some portals into Cyberspace have been almost completely closed to Chinese citizens, such as Facebook, which is rapidly becoming a global community and source for widescale cultural diffusion.

The motivations for governments to intervene in Cyberspace are multiple. The Communist Party of China (CPC), which has a firm grip on the PRC government and shows no signs of abandoning the authoritarian model it has deployed in governing China since 1949, seeks to retain at least a modicum of control over the information available to Chinese citizens, at least the vast majority of the citizenry that does not have the ability to seek education, work, or other social life outside of the boundaries of the PRC. The ban on Facebook shows that the greatest fear is that Chinese citizens might have a means for mass organization (the epitome of the rising technomass), which could always turn political and pose a direct threat to CPC authority, even putting some truth to the "People's Republic" adjective. At present, the code governing Cyberspace is at odds with the code embodied in Chinese governmental authority over Chinese citizens, creating a contradiction that the Chinese government is intent upon resolving in its favor and can only do so by either forging alliances with transnational corporate structures, forcing these corporate structures to cooperate, or developing CPC-controlled or influenced domestic corporate structures with the power to act as intermediaries between Chinese citizens and Cyberspace. For example, in the world of search engines, a key nexus connecting citizens to Cyberspace, Google is globally dominant but has been a bit of a pain in the backside for the Chinese government, and within China an alternative search engine, Baidu, has a dominant market share. Baidu toes the CPC line and makes sure that searches result in more acceptable results than might be expected from the American firm, Google.

The reality is that the CPC has very little actual power over Google or Microsoft or Yahoo or any number of other transnational firms. These corporate structures can be coerced, perhaps, by the threat of losing licenses and therefore access to the Chinese market (at least in part, since the technomass will, most certainly, circumvent most of the attempts at total control or restriction of access) but it is just as likely that these firms will find ways to cooperate because they perceive it in their interest to do so, even if they protest that they are being coerced. In other words, the interest of these nation-states and some of the corporate structures may ultimately coincide and be at odds with the interests of the rising technomass. After all, the evolution of the nation-state and corporate structures has coincided (the latter is an offspring of the former). The rising technomass is an accidental mutation within cultural evolution as a result of a complex array of technological advances, a socio-technological structure without structure (in the sense of predesigned outcomes or telos), generating its own rules on the fly, and dependent upon a radical form of democratic and always contingent participation and agreement among the members. The culture generated by the technomass, precisely because it is so radically democratic, so anarchistic, is naturally a threat to hierarchical power structures. At the end of the day, the rising technomass may not find many allies among either nation-states or large scale corporate structures. The fact that the technomass is capable of large scale organization without authority and, therefore, the potential to trigger revolutionary change in any country at any time, is reason enough for existing authority structures to be concerned and to seek ways to dampen or block the effects of this sort of cooperation, if not to smash the technomass altogether.

This leads to the question of whether this new social structure that has evolved, the rising technomass, can force these older structures to change and accommodate? Alternatively, the authoritarian governmental and corporate structures may recognize the threat and either alter the rules of the economic and technological game or find ways to change (innovate) in ways that regenerate their own power over social relationships and modes of communication, including by taking control over the use of Cyberspace, to the detriment of further evolution of the technomass (or even in ways that lead to the destruction of the technomass) and, perhaps, even stymie larger cultural evolution of the human species? It would certainly not be the first time that narrow self interest served to stunt human economic and cultural development. Despite the usual rhetoric that capitalism has been the source of all that is good and great about life in the 21st century, one does not know what alternative modes of social organization could have achieved. It is not enough to point to the few examples of, generally, more authoritarian political systems (Stephen Resnick and Richard Wolff provide a well argued case that the Soviet Union was unambiguously an example of a variant form of capitalist society, namely state capitalism, rather than an alternative to capitalism, as many have argued, usually without the sort of careful analysis found in Resnick and Wolff's work) to say that we live in the best of all possible worlds. This is just an extreme case of survivorship bias combining with parochialism. The alternative social systems never explored could, very well, have been vastly superior to the choices made, resulting in higher quality of life for humanity, reducing risks of environmental or social disasters, fostering more nurturing relationships, etc. If social technology is similar to material technology, there is no reason to believe such is not the case. It has, generally, only been in the crucible of social crises that revolutionary changes in social systems have occurred and, even then, it is rare. Most of the time (and both the USSR and the PRC are cases in point) the changes that occurred post-revolution were largely changes in the elite that controlled social institutions, many, if not most, of which predated the revolution.

The rise of the technomass, on the other hand, represents something truly revolutionary and its rise is a genuine threat to authoritarian power. Thus, the struggle is on. The old system will fight to survive and the new system will move chaotically in any space allowed it. Whether the technomass will play a critical role in altering the existing complex of power and privilege remains to be seen.

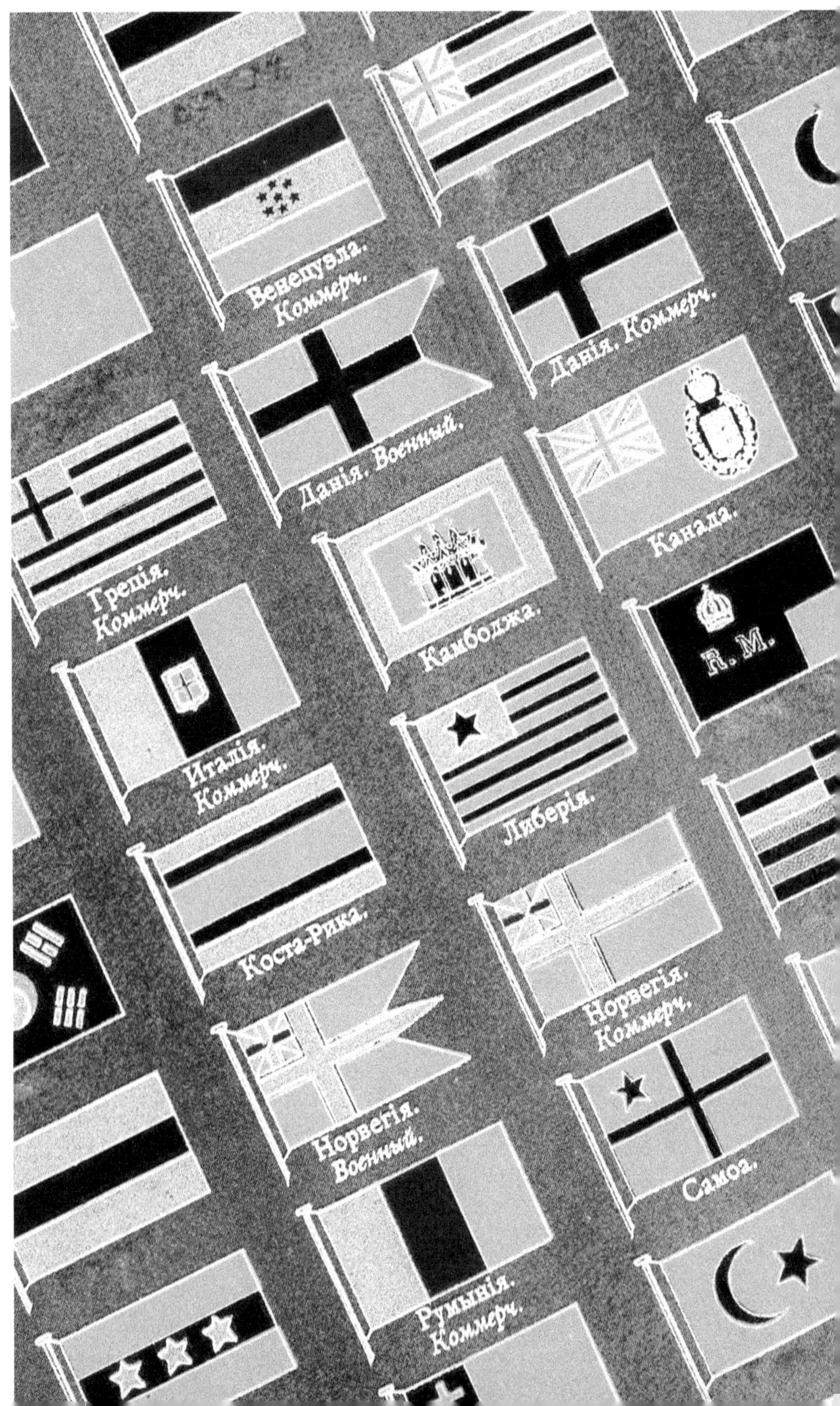
Венецуэла.
Коммерч.
Данія. Коммерч.
Данія. Военный.
Канада.
Греція.
Коммерч.
Камбоджа.
R. M.
Италія.
Коммерч.
Либерія.
Коста-Рика.
Норвегія.
Коммерч.
Норвегія.
Военный.
Самоа.
Румынія.
Коммерч.

the (r)evolution
of social formations
beyond nation-states,
beyond the constraints
and
conceits
of nationalism
has become
a possibility:

the creation of a
boundary-less

humanity.

Cyberspace is revolutionary because it represents an interconnected web of technologies that is shaped to maximize the spontaneous interaction of human beings utilizing those tools. It allows relatively unmediated interactions across vast geographic space and with very little in the way of time cost. The most powerful aspect of this new technological gestalt is the way it provides for an enormous space for interactions, with little in the way of limitation on the number of participants, the quantity of data exchanged, and the degree to which diffusion of knowledge is facilitated. The creation of Cyberspace obliterated a number of boundaries that had limited the speed and extent of human cultural evolution. The rising technomass represents a spontaneous attempt to innovate within that space, to take full advantage of the power of these new technologies and the Cyberspace created by them to push human cultural evolution forward. Now the limitations we face are largely the result of state and corporate interventions into Cyberspace.

Cyberspace transcends the limitations of geography, allowing for social interaction to occur between actors whose physical bodies are separated by vast distances and for the transmission of information instantly without immediate human intervention. As Brinkman points out in *Cultural Economics*, knowledge is the substance of human cultural evolution. Knowledge is the raw material and the diffusion of knowledge the motor for economic development. Therefore, to the extent Cyberspace facilitates the collaborative development of new knowledge through both the efforts of traditional institutions and the rising technomass, it also facilitates, indeed propels forward, economic development. Efforts to stymie this process of knowledge diffusion, such as through blocking websites, censorship, restrictions on the use of technologies that allow for greater knowledge diffusion, etc. place limitations on economic development and human progress. Potentially the cost could be incalculable because the progress of human cultural evolution is the key to human species survival. If we learn at a slower pace, if cultural evolution is slowed by the interventions of selfish actors with inordinate powers over the advance of Cyberspace, then we will not invent and innovate fast enough to meet the serious challenges of the present and uncertain future, whether in the form of global climate change, approaching asteroids, or mutating viruses. In other words, the struggle to keep Cyberspace relatively "free" may be a life or death struggle. If closed source prevails, if net neutrality dies, if the Great Firewall of China succeeds, we could all pay the ultimate price...

extinction.

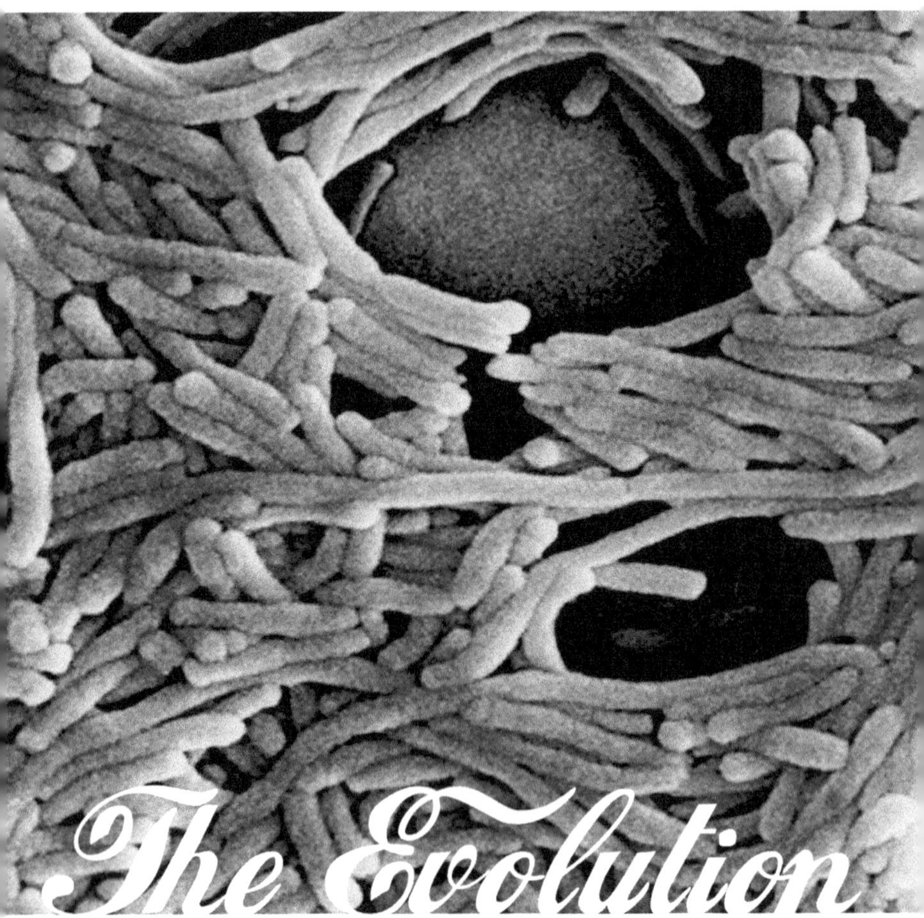

The Evolution

FREE ACCESS TO KNOWLEDGE WAS ONCE THE

KNOWLEDGE WAS ONCE THE CLOSELY GUARDED

FOR WHOM BOUNDARIES WERE MOMENTARY

IN THE 21ST CENTURY THE KNOWLEDGE WALL IS

PRIVILEGED ACCESS IS DIFFICULT TO PROTECT

THE MASSES HAVE BECOME WIRED

THIS IS THE AGE OF THE DECENTRALIZED TECHNOMASSES

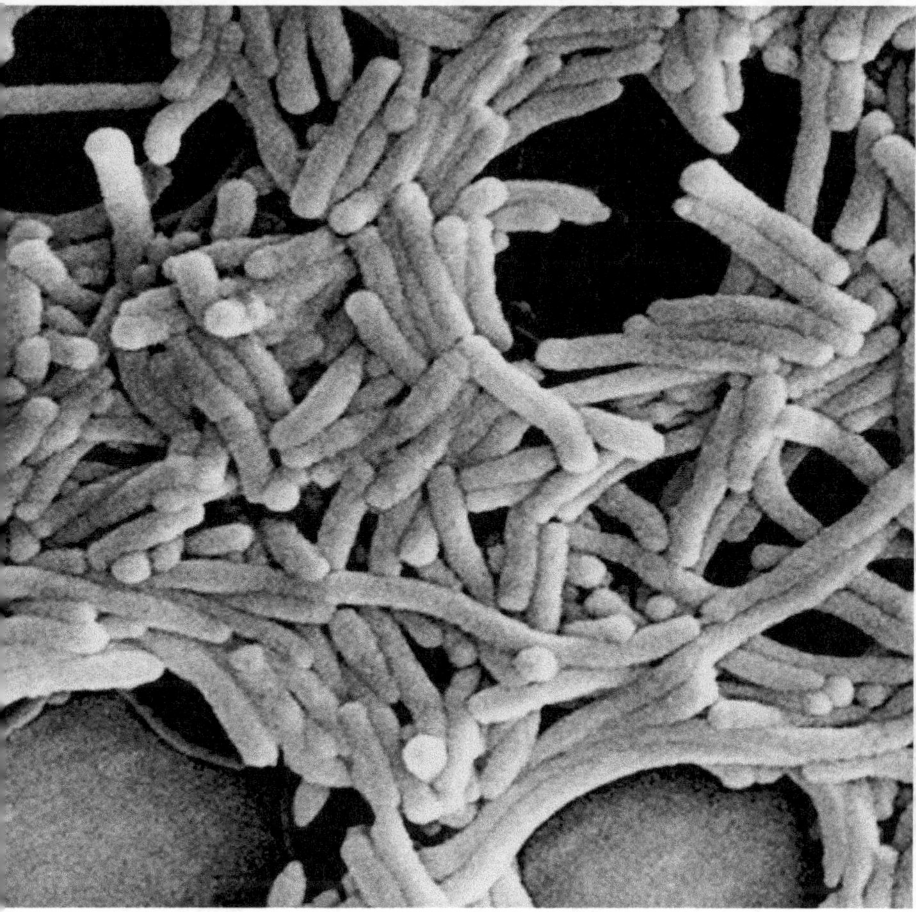

SUBJECT OF FICTIONS AND FANTASIES

RIGHT OF THE FEW AND THE PRIVILEGED

INCONVENIENCES EASILY OVERCOME

TORN DOWN BY TECHNOLOGICAL MEANS

WHEN EVERYONE HAS A KEY

FOR LIBERATION FROM CENTRALIZED HIERARCHIES

BARRIERS ARE DISINTEGRATING

we all have a fundamental need to discover, that which is unknown to us; we decipher the wholeness underneath the fragmented. the outlook of our existence is defined by how we choose to connect to others. reality is articulated by rapidly changing paradigms; the rigid and dogmatic will be left behind; our actions, guided by interacting thoughts within the evolving Technomass, craft a rapidly transforming mix of services, goods, cyber-institutions, cyber-economies, and tools for social engagement that govern our interrelation with reality. we are in flux. we are technologies employing other technologies to assemble, shape, and reshape a coherent story (out of the chaos of evolution) about our own condition.

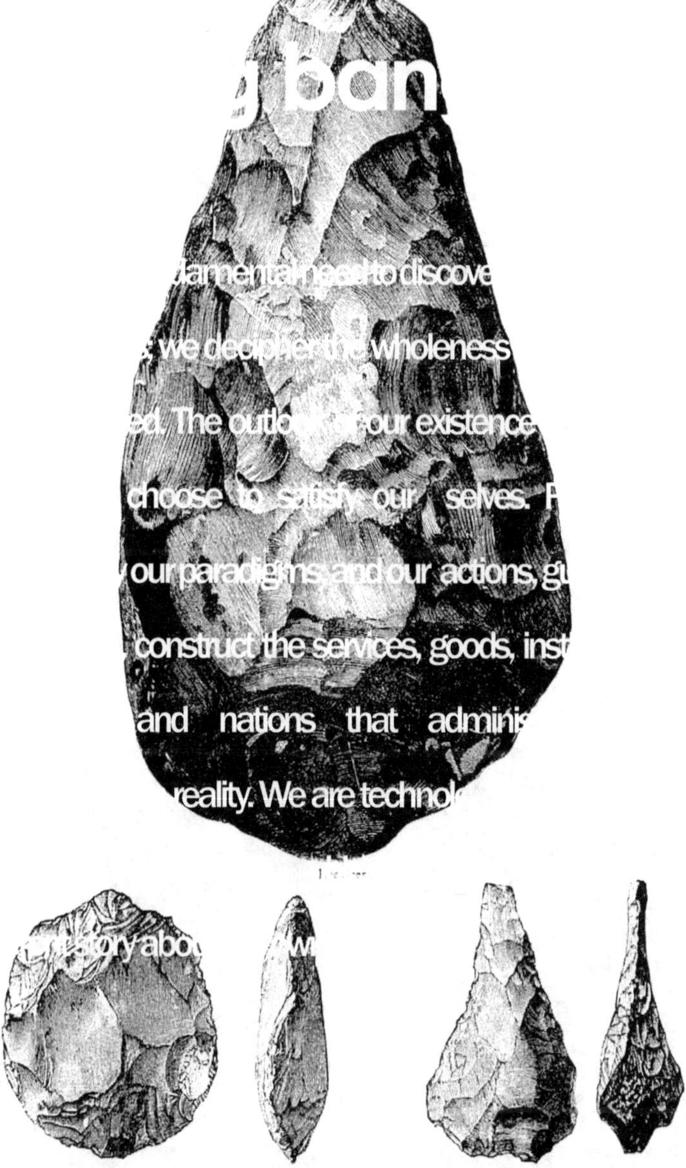

Bewley, Ightham. Reculver.

Palæolithic Implements found in Kent.

TECHNOLOGY DISCLOSES THE ACTIVE RELATION OF MAN TOWARDS NATURE, AS WELL AS THE DIRECT PROCESS OF PRODUCTION OF HIS VERY LIFE, AND

Capitalism depends on the exploitation of human talent and energy by those in a privileged position to control the technology required for creating new value. The decentralization of technology has opened the door to everyone being an entrepreneur. The market has been liberated from capitalism.

THEREBY THE PROCESS
OF PRODUCTION OF
HIS BASIC SOCIETAL
RELATIONS, OF HIS OWN
MENTALITY, AND HIS
IMAGES OF SOCIETY, TOO.

-Karl Marx-

individual freedom:

interacting through media:
interacting with and changing code
within
networked information economies
linking you
to everyone else
can become
the regulating force
behind the evolutionary flow of our society

5

Conditions of Existence

This text is part of a larger project to rethink the role of technology in shaping culture and the role of culture in generating new technics. Technology is and has always been an expression of human creativity in the face of the challenges posed by the natural and social environment. This is no less true of that set of technologies that have unleashed an information technology revolution at the end of the 20th century and continue to this day: a revolutionary new environment for human communication and the diffusion of knowledge that has been called Cyberspace.

Cyberspace is predicated upon a series of prior advances in technology and upon determinate social relationships by which those technologies were first adopted and then allowed to diffuse within various social formations. These technologies include telegraphic, telephonic, and eventually electronic communications systems, radio and television transmission systems, and the development of computer systems. The technologies that predated Cyberspace were primarily oriented around either moving data between individual communication nodes (two telephones mediated by the larger telecommunications network) or from one node to multiple nodes (as in the case of one-way signal transmission, such as the broadcasting of television signals). Although the potential for transforming these early systems into something comparable to Cyberspace existed, the impediments to doing so were both technological and social. Indeed, in the early history of television there were those who believed this device would become a two way communications device that might facilitate the mass diffusion of knowledge, but this was not pursued in a context where the development of television for commercial purposes was steered towards one way transmission of advertising messages from a central source to a passive mass of individual watchers/listeners. The development of Cyberspace is singularly revolutionary in introducing for the first time a technological gestalt oriented around mass communication and knowledge diffusion. The fact that the technologies have been developed in a manner that minimizes the need for controlling the flows of information/communication is critical to the potentials that are embedded within this space.

Ironically, this anarchic nature of Cyberspace may have been deliberately engineered by the most hierarchical of institutional structures, the military, in particular the U.S. military. The U.S. military sought to find a technological means of maintaining the flow of communication and data transmission under potentially catastrophic circumstances and the development of an open system, i.e. Cyberspace, provided a solution to this problem. Thus, the creation of an anarchistic realm of communications and information flow, Cyberspace, may have been dependent upon the actions of an institutional structure that was the diametrical opposite of the anarchist's dream and the creation of one of the most anarchist-friendly social spaces ever devised was, to a significant extent, the brainchild of scientists and engineers working for the military. This may be one of the most glaring examples of the law of unintended consequences in practice.

The military's role in developing the early technological infrastructure may have been important, but the role of academic scientists would be even more critical to the establishment, in the early 1980s, of a common set of codes for communication between the various early networks set up for sharing data across communities of proto-techno-masses, mostly comprised of academics at research universities eager both to engage colleagues and to advance an exciting new form of technology. The development and advance of generic code protocols has continued to be a key condition for the existence and advance of Cyberspace.

The 1990s is the decade when the proto-techno-masses would evolve into the technomass, as the technologies for accessing Cyberspace became available to individuals beyond the research campuses, allowing the process of code writing and sharing, and experimentation to become relatively pervasive. The democratization of Cyberspace is critical to the explosive growth in these technologies and the transformation of Cyberspace into a competing realm of mass social interaction and creativity. It also provided the basis for transforming a largely intellectual environment into one where the multiplicity of human interactions could occur, including, quite consequentially, commercial and financial transactions that made it possible to generate new forms of value and inaugurate new types of business enterprises. Cyberspace has thus evolved into a sphere of social life in a more total sense than was ever envisioned by its pioneers and may even someday largely displace the physical realm as the preferred space for all sorts of human interactions. This can already be glimpsed in the sharp increase in time spent within Cyberspace. In a matter of less than 20 years, Cyberspace has evolved from an interesting curiousity to a vital aspect of most people's lives.

The challenge we face is to recognize that the growing importance of Cyberspace also makes it likely that the extraordinary freedoms experienced within that space may be undermined by institutions that are threatened by this migration of human interaction from a physical realm that was easier to control into this digital space that is grounded in anarchistic relationships. Cyberspace represents a genuine threat to centralized authorities of all types, including, but not restricted to, authoritarian governments. However, it is this very anarchy that is the strength of Cyberspace, providing human beings with the rare freedom to create and to communicate without mediators. In this regard, Cyberspace may appear to some as a real world manifestation of that most illusive of ideas, a utopia, at least in terms of the realization of humankind's long sought after quest for genuine freedom.

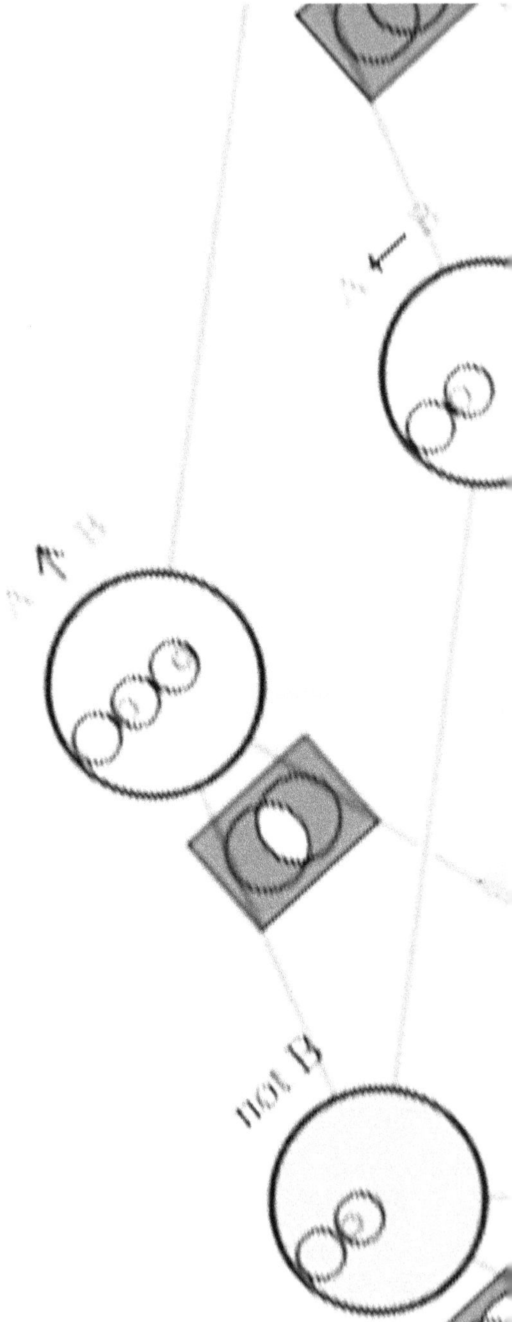

implications.

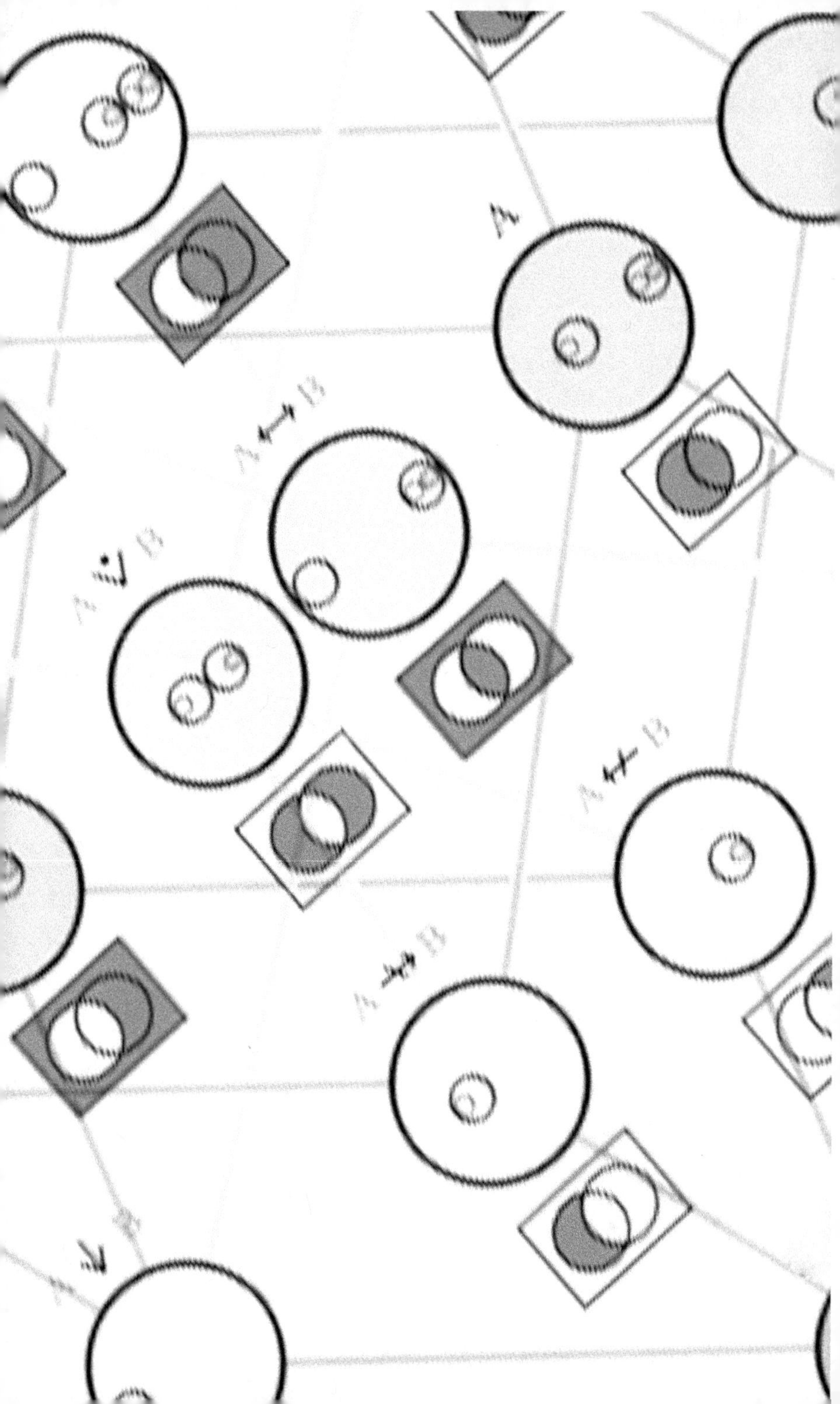

6

It is not uncommon for books, movies, and, especially television to portray invention as a process by which an inspired genius invents something extraordinary, something disconnected from all prior inventions or knowledge. Science fiction (loosely defined) is often constructed around such a notion of invention. This idea is probably one of the most harmful fantasies when it comes to invention and innovation, only superceded by the argument that these inspired inventions should rightfully be owned by a corporate entity with the right to restrict access to the underlying blueprints or codes. The truth is very different. No one invents out of thin air. Inspiration is always a function of putting together ideas already known in a novel way. Technology has always been the result of collaborative processes between those occupying the present moment and all those who came at earlier moments and left a legacy of ideas (also the product of the past).

Human beings invent by combining available knowledge in new ways. Available knowledge has been open source for most of human history, meaning that anyone who could gain access to the knowledge had the right and sometimes even the obligation to use it. The state or religious institutions acting as pseudo-state agencies attempted to restrict access to knowledge but, except for limited cases, did not attempt to confer ownership of the knowledge. Knowledge was something very different from a material object that could be possessed as property, sometimes viewed as spiritual and always understood as immaterial. This way of thinking served humankind well, providing the basis for our exponential rise in technological capability.

One of the extraordinary aspects of arguments in favor of expanding and intensifying property rights in the digital realm is that it requires a dramatic increase in governmental authority within that realm for enforcement. Expanding the powers of the state carries risks, which should be clear to anyone with even a passing knowledge of the history of political economy. Do we really want to increase the size and scope and power of the state such that it can monitor our communications and work within Cyberspace? If so, what is to say that these powers will not ultimately come back to haunt us, including placing governmental power in the way of the innovativeness that is the hallmark of life within Cyberspace?

The primary contemporary argument in favor of expanding the role of the state to policing code (i.e. specific arrangements of concepts and logical connections between concepts) is grounded in the idea that ownership of code/knowledge (as opposed to ownership of physical artifacts created from code) is a prerequisite to further innovation. The argument is simple:

1. Creative work is essential to the functioning of society.

2. Creative work will not occur if it is not compensated. Thus, the rate of innovation is directly and positively correlated to the probability

and amount of compensation received by creative workers.

3. Creative work can only be compensated by the receipt of income in the form of cash payments to the creative agent or the employer of the creative agent. In order for IPR held by corporations to satisfy the conditions of the argument, one needs to add the clause whereby corporations that employ creative workers are the recepients of the relevant cash flows.

4. The creative agent or her/his employer will be unable to gain these cash payments without having ownership of (exclusive use rights to) the code embodied in the creative work. Again, it doesn't matter whether the product innovator directly receives payment or is simply paid a salary by a corporation that owns the IPR and receives the direct payments for IPR. If one assumed that the product designer/innovator needed to directly receive the value of her/his creations, then the current (capitalist) IPR regime could be considered defective because the corporation receives a substantially larger compensation for IPR than the relatively small share of the IPR embodied in the salaries of the creative staff. In other words, it is necessary to ignore capitalist exploitation to make the philosophical case for the currently prevalent IPR regime.

5. Intellectual property rights (IPR) is the appropriate form of ownership embodied in legal codes enforceable by the state. To reiterate what was stated above, a Marxian analysis of IPR

would argue for an IPR regime that grants these rights to the direct producers of innovation. The product designers and engineers who created the iPhone, for example, would own the patents rather than Apple, Inc. Similarly, and perhaps more to the point of the current debate, the director, writers, actors, and other creative talent who create motion pictures would own the IPR to those motion pictures, rather than Disney or Time Warner or any other corporate entity.

6. IPR enforcement must include the restriction of use rights to the owner or those who have paid the owner of the IPR for the transfer of such rights. In the case of corporate ownership of IPR, these restrictions apply to the direct producers of the innovation (as paid employees of the IPR owner, they have no rights to the IPR and are subject to legal action for distributing or otherwise using the IPR without the express permission of corporate management).

7. All other uses of the intellectual property (in the form of specific code) must be subject to legal action and related judgments or punishments sufficient to guarantee the integrity of IPR.

There are several problems with this logic. Firstly, doesn't history show us clearly that creative work occurs, in many, if not most, instances for non-pecuniary reasons? The conundrum presented by the Open Source Movement, at least from the standpoint of mainstream economic theory, is that countless individuals gift their creative work to a mass movement over which they have no ultimate control. Indeed, this mass movement is precisely what we refer to herein as the technomass.

Furthermore, the granting of IPR is predicated on compensating the source of creative output, but no creative work occurs in isolation and someone is always uncompensated. Family, friends, and associates may contribute in a wide variety of ways to the development of an idea. Perhaps most importantly, in all instances, there were past creative individuals who go uncompensated but whose creative output is embodied in the work of the agent granted the IPR. Thus, from an economic standpoint, the real social cost of creative work is never fully reflected in IPR. Humans are social beings (not autonomous, atomistic individuals) and this is reflected in the advance of human knowledge and the material technics generated from that knowledge.

And, perhaps most critically, if it is correct that knowledge diffusion generates greater inventions and innovations, then restrictions on knowledge diffusion run counter to the typically stated social/economic objective of IPR. This would particularly be the case if the IPR is granted for process code (such as an operating system or the rights to make and use a musical instrument, which is the tool for carrying out creative processes by which new products and/or technics are generated).

As authors of this text, we are not opponents of the rights of creative individuals to be recognized and rewarded. We celebrate this creativity and recognize that it is precisely what makes humans distinct on this planet, our extraordinary creativity. We think it would be just to recognize every person who contributes new inventions or new modes of cultural expression to humanity, as it would be to recognize those who help to foster such creativity. But is this really the point of the IPR debate? As Bowles and Gintis pointed out in their 1986 text, *Democracy & Capitalism*, the implementation of property laws was never really about protecting property rights per se but was, rather, "a movement toward the treatment of property law as an arm of accumulation" favoring capitalist corporate structures over individuals, including or especially artists and other creative workers.

The state and the laws that legitimize state coercive power have served and continue to serve as a means of securing the conditions for the continued accumulation of capital within large-scale corporate structures that also serve as vessels within which creative individuals are exploited by being only partially compensated for the valuable output they generate. Because the products sold by these corporate structures incorporate intellectual "property" secured from the larger store of human culture without compensating anyone (a form of theft, in IPR terms), then it can also be said that the accumulation process depends upon not only the exploitation of internal creative workers but the exploitation of human culture, as a whole. Legal regimes provide the justification and enforcement of the rights to carry out this exploitation and to restrain other agents from interfering in such exploitation. Although the general attitude seems to have been that "resistance is futile" in the face of the combined power of mega-corporate structures and a powerful state judicial and law enforcement bureaucracy, the technomass has formed, in part, as just such a force of resistance.

Thus, the point is simply that efforts to bound code/knowledge to favor accumulation via draconian laws that restrict individual rights are likely to backfire, to slow economic progress *and* spark strong resistance from the technomasses who have gained access to tools that circumvent centralized control over code. Those using these tools include creative workers, including musicians and visual artists, the very body of individuals who are often cited as the beneficiaries of IPR and the victims of the technomass.

The Technomass has become all the more strongly oppositional to the power of states and allied corporate structures to restrict access to code and the rewriting of code because the attempts to enforce IPR have been perceived as both severely authoritarian and Luddite. Some elements of the Technomass resist all forms of IPR. Most resist only those attempts by the state to close access to those process codes that are necessary for creative work and unreasonable restrictions on the use of code.

However, it is unclear that there is a widespread understanding within the technomass that the current IPR regime favors capitalist accumulation at the expense of the rights of individuals to creative expression through the manipulation and sharing of code, as well as remixing processes that take as raw material prior creative outputs, rather than a more libertarian or anarchist rejection of centralized political authority over the activities of code writers and users. It may very well be the case that the technomass has created a libertarian/anarchist subculture within Cyberspace and the technomass is, in part, an expression of this subculture.

The reaction against authority within the technomass may be only in part a cultural expression of the new technologies by which Cyberspace was born and is reproduced, technologies that have allowed individuals to unite in a variety of new ways to carry out creative activities. The libertarian/anarchist aspect of the technomass may also be yet another form of reaction against the ever expanding bureaucratic nature of capitalist society, where corporate structures dominate all forms of social life. In this sense, the technomass could be a younger sibling of other post-capitalist social movements, such as the beatnik and hippie cultures of the 20th century, both of which had artistic elements and both of which can be seen as influencing various cultural expressions within the tech community, particularly among programmers and gamers.

In this context, Abbie Hoffman's reprise of Proudhon's "property is theft" resonates. On the other hand, the claim that is made by supporters of the existing IPR regime that the problem is "theft" of creative products with the result that humanity may suffer a diminution in creative output requires acceptance of a one-sided argument about corporate ownership rights and ignores the violations of the rights of countless creative individuals, as well as collectives outside the capitalist corporate sphere, who have created the raw material employed to generate corporate revenues but are not provided with either compensation or protections within this existing regime.

The contradictions in the existing IPR regime are widely recognized within the technomass, despite pervasive propaganda in support of that regime and against those within the technomass who violate it on a regular basis. This challenge to the state and allied corporate structures may, potentially, have larger implications. If enforcement of an IPR regime that is so widely recognized as "unfair" exposes the relationship between the state and allied corporate structures as one that is opposed to democratic processes (with the state seen as a captive of those corporate structures, despite the electoral processes associated with democratic selection of representatives), then this struggle could lead more individuals (particularly those who have grown up as, at least in part, members of the rising technomass) to an oppositional politics against the larger accumulation regime, of which the IPR regime is only a small part, that shapes so much of social life in the 21st century.

if you understand the coding behind the technologies that define our lives in this new era you will be able to adapt your possibilities and creativity to the Technomass and use it to your advantage .

those who fail to understand the coding and implications of these technologies must, nevertheless, adapt, but will lose control to the black box computing/cyberaccess machines, and have no choice but to deal with the economic and social consequences/ surprises

those of us who understand the coding behind the technologies that define our lives in this new epoch will be able to correctly adapt our possibilities and limitations to the technomass and use it to our advantage.

those of us who fail to understand the coding and implications of these technologies will simply have no choice but to adapt as best one can, to the black box computing/cyberspaces machines, and deal with the economic and social consequences/surprises

Humanity in the techno forest

The forces of change are overdetermined:
too complex to decipher. those who seek to regulate the forest, exert authority over it, will find their task complicated by the very nature of the environment where every single moment produces innovations to circumvent their efforts at control.

there is no cyber-apocalypse coming any time soon. the emerging Technomass is only one of countless interacting and interdependent factors reshaping the norms that govern behavior in our social formations. the complex interplay of changing technologies with political, cultural, environmental, and economic processes generates new possibilities for individual and social identities. entrepreneurs will find new ways to serve the needs and wants of these new identities. new markets are emerging within cyberspace and old markets are being challenged. some business models have become obsolete. other business models have risen from fantasy to practicality. as Joseph Schumpeter pointed out, creative destruction is the name of the game in the entrepreneurial battle for survival and success. how we embrace this gestalt today will determine the opportunities for generations to come.

INDIVIDUAL NATION-STATES

AND

CORPORATIONS

MUST ADJUST RAPIDLY

OR FACE FAILURE.

RISK IS THE INABILITY TO ADJUST

TO CHANGE IN TIME.

TIME IS SHRINKING.

INSTITUTIONS THAT ARE

UNABLE

TO TAKE ADVANTAGE OF

THE TRANSFORMATIONS

GENERATED BY

TECHNOLOGY

ARE LIKELY TO

DISAPPEAR

(VERY SOON)

THE PERCEPTION, OFTEN PRESENTED BY SOCIAL SCIENTISTS, THAT SOCIETY IS A STATIC PHENOMENON IS AN ILLUSION. NOTHING REMAINS THE SAME. NO EQUILIBRIA EXIST. EVERYTHING EXISTS IN FLUX. EVERYTHING IS A FORM OF CHANGING TECHNOLOGY, INCLUDING US. IF ONE ELEMENT IN THE GESTALT CHANGES THEN ALL ELEMENTS CHANGE. THIS IS THE NATURE OF REALITY. EVERYTHING IS CODE. DNA. KNOWLEDGE. THE COSMOS. EVERYTHING IS IN FLUX. THE CLOCK IS OVERDETERMINED BY THE SOCIETY WHICH IS RADICALLY DYNAMIC. HERACLITUS WAS RIGHT ON.

THE SHARING OF KNOWLEDGE IS A FUNDAMENTAL LAW OF LIFE. DNA IS OPEN SOURCE. HUMANITY (OUR CULTURE, OUR BIOLOGY) IS THE END RESULT OF A LONG (IN BOTH TEMPORAL AND SPATIAL TERMS) OPEN SOURCE PROJECT.

"Any sufficiently advanced technology is indistinguishable from magic"

—Arthur C. Clarke

synthetic nature

DMT (Ayahuasca) · LSD · Mescaline (Peyote, San Pedro) · Psilocybin (Magic Mushrooms) **D**issociatives DXM · Inhalants · Ketamine · Nitrous Oxide · PCP · Salvinorin A (Salvia) **D**eliriants Datura · Deadly Nightshade · Henbane · Mandrake **O**pioids Codeine · Heroin · Hydrocodone · Morphine (Opium) · Oxycodone **S**timulants Amphetamine · Arecoline (Areca) · Betel · Caffeine (Coffee, Tea) · Cathinone (Khat) · Cocaine (Coca) · Ephedrine (Ephedra) · Methamphetamine · Methylphenidate · Nicotine (Tobacco) · Theobromine (Cocoa)

001000000111011101101111

101110010011011000110010

000111001100100000001101

organic nature

010111001100100000011001

110110111101101001011011

100110011100100000001110

100011011111001000000110

001101101000011000010110

111001100111011001010010

000001101001011011100010

000001110111011000010110

110010111001100100000011

010000100000011101010110

111001100100011001010111

001001110011011110100011

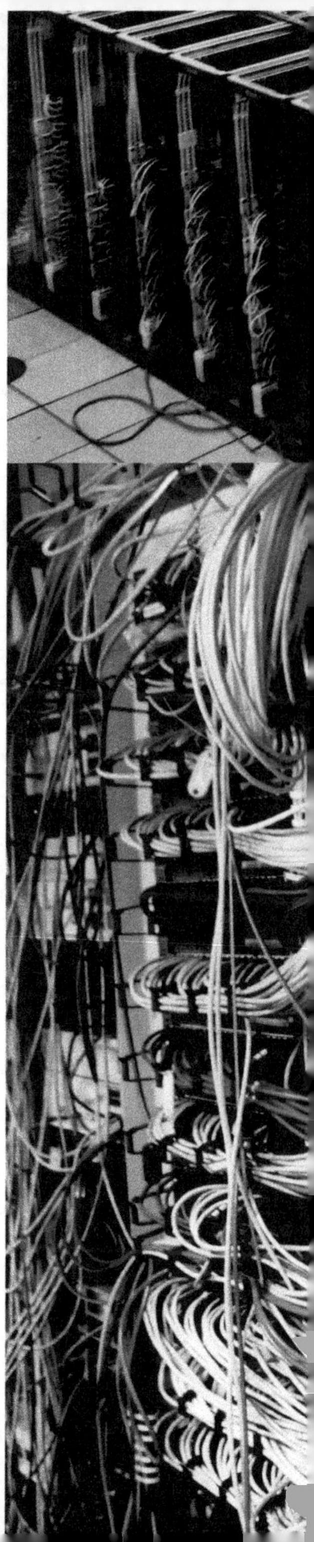

"A hen is only an egg's way of making another egg"
—Samuel Butler

BREAK THE EGGS AND MAKE A SUPER BIRD.

Birth of the Decentralized Technomass

Birth of a new society where access to information and power is radically diffused within communities

THE POTENTIAL IN THE NEW COMBINATION OF AUTONOMOUS INDIVIDUALS, CYBER-COMMUNITIES, AND TECHNOLOGICAL MEANS OF INSTANTANEOUS AND VIRTUALLY UNMEDIATED COMMUNICATION IS FAR MORE THAN APPEARANCES WOULD INDICATE. IT IS, IN APPEARANCE, LIKE THE EGG. JUST AS AN EGG CAN HARBOR SOMETHING FAR GREATER THAN ITSELF, THE NEW TECHNOMASS MAY HOLD THE SUBSTANCE TO A FAR GREATER FORM OF SOCIETY: A SUPER SOCIAL FORMATION THAT FINALLY LIBERATES HUMAN TALENT AND CREATIVITY FROM THE CONSTRAINTS OF HIERARCHY, PRIVILEGE, AND BUREAUCRATIC CONTROL.

The Decline of the Holy Trinity: Mega-Banks Mega-Industrial Corporations and Nation-states

STOCK EXCHANGE

7

Capitalism has developed over the past two hundred years into a system that pervades all aspects of social life. Indeed, this system, grounded in the deployment of armies of wage laborers under the command of trained managers, and a bureaucratic system whose linkages touch nearly every other economic, political, and cultural institution, especially government, has so insinuated itself into the life and consciousness of the citizenry as to become virtually invisible. The rising technomass, however, highlights the differences between that social structure founded upon capitalist hierarchy and authority and a newly evolved system of social interaction based on genuine freedom of action, relative autonomy, and cooperation within a relatively egalitarian and certainly meritocratic sphere.

The rising technomass is a force that challenges the capitalist paradigm that dominates the economic sphere of social life (capitalism defined not in terms of "free markets" but capitalism as Marx defined it—a system based on exploitation of free wage labor, as opposed to the self-employment of independent producers or communal workers, as in the kibbutz system, and also distinguised from other forms of exploitative economic systems, such as slavery and feudalism) and the authoritarian political paradigm that continues to dominate social life in many countries and has legacy effects even in democratic societies, particularly where corporate power has displaced the power of the citizenry to shape social life and the rules of the political, cultural, and economic games. Formation and expansion of the technomass represents a significant rupture from the trend towards corporate power in both the economic and political sphere. In the former, corporate power has come to dominate through control over household incomes and the choices households have available for consumption and lifestyles. Most people work for corporations and their jobs are a condition for their normal existence, including access to shelter, food, clothing, health care, and a wide range of other necessities of social life. Young people learn very early in life that they must conform to corporate requirements if they are to be chosen for employment and have access to the commodities necessary to this normal existence. To be employed and to have access to commodities may also shape a person's self-image and their ability to secure desirable relationships with others. To the extent capitalism presents the individual with the alternative (real or perceived) between working in a wage labor setting and being an outsider in this system without access to life's necessities is the extent capitalism is a social system that captures the hearts and minds and becomes self-reproducing, minimizing resistance or even criticism. This system works much better than slavery because the "brainwashing" is self-applied. You learn to make yourself over so as to be perceived as a good employment candidate and later, after having been hired, to be perceived as a good employee,to avoid being fired or passed over for promotion. Unlike slavery or feudalism, where resistance to exploitation could arise out of the stark reality of being directly controlled/coerced, capitalism offers an illusion of individual choice and freedom of choice: the individual employee having chosen their fate and having the freedom to change that fate anytime they want. Who would one rebel against under such an arrangement, yourself?

The technomass, however, has served to unveil this system for many people. Cyberspace offers a contrast to the capitalist spaces, where genuine freedom to make one's own choices, to interact with others in creative ways without the intermediary of corporate structures, to be entrepreneurs without the need for large capital outlays that might be available to only a select few. Participants in Cyberspace recognize the contrast with corporate life, where control is in other people's hands and, given corporate dynamics, sometimes seems to be embedded in an impersonal bureaucratic structure for which no one takes ultimate responsibility. The concept of autonomy/freedom takes on a more tangible form in Cyberspace, while it largely serves as empty rhetoric when applied to capitalism. The more participation in the technomass teaches this lesson, the more dangerous this formation becomes for capitalism. The same is true for authoritarian political structures (including the political organization of corporate structures). Authoritarian governments should be particularly concerned with the rising technomass. The link between individuals is being forged in Cyberspace without intermediation by the state, allowing for coordination of political action, exposure of government hypocrisy, corruption and other misdeeds, and for forging alliances across geographic and demographic spaces previously serving as barriers to mass organization and resistance. Authoritarian regimes will fall in the face of the rising technomass. Corporate structures will have to adapt by becoming more open and flexible, less dogmatic and authoritarian, or they will face a similar fate.

If you open a typical undergraduate economics textbook, you are likely to encounter some version of Lionel Robbins's 1932 definition of the discipline as "the science which studies human behaviour as a relationship between ends and scarce means which have alternative uses." In addition to excluding a wide range of concerns of economists over the history of the discipline, including questions of income distribution, economic exploitation, and role of institutions in shaping the life choices and chances of individuals and their kinship groups, this notion of scarcity is linked to the idea of physical resources and presumes limitations to access and use of resources. While the artifacts of human knowledge are typically physical objects, knowledge is, in and of itself, intangible and less subject to physical limitations of access and use. Knowledge exists as concepts and logic. As such, knowledge is non-rival and transferable from human to human, even from one human to masses of humans.

The canon

Unlike a physical apple, the "consumption" of knowledge is not a zero sum game—we can share without losing access ourselves. Sharing of knowledge has benefited humanity immensely, is, perhaps, the very nature of humanity. In this sense, the neoclassical paradigm begins by ignoring what makes humans different from the vast majority

of other lifeforms on the planet Earth. In doing so, the neoclassical paradigm loses the ability to understand human evolution, the dynamics of human society, and the key role that knowledge plays in shaping not only our decision sets as individual human beings but the context of those decisions.

However, the neoclassical paradigm is indoctrinated in most economists, often long before they select the discipline as their specialty. Nowadays the neoclassical doctrine is regularly taught in high schools, often to even younger students, before these individuals have experienced enough life to reject the doctrine as unrealistic. Economists trained in the doctrine have gained sufficient power within the discipline to exclude all other forms of economic thought and have secured a monopoly in the teaching of introductory economics, such that even "heterodox" economists are forced to teach the doctrine. How is technology understood within the doctrine? It is understood as a functional relationship between inputs and outputs. This is really the mindset of capitalism, where human creativity and energy is nothing more than labor time units that are bought and sold in "labor markets," just like apples and oranges are sold in apple and orange markets. There is no understanding of the fundamentally technological context of human creativity and energy. Human beings are biological machines but are more than that. Human beings have the ability to innovate new forms of technology, including soft forms of technology, in the form of relationships, by which we act to transform the world. There is really no other "input" that has this ability and there is no equation that captures the innovative nature of human work or the unique nature of each and every human worker/creator. The neoclassical paradigm, by reducing human beings to inputs, misses a key point of economics. Human beings placed in an environment that allows full play of their creative ability will change everything, be productive in ways that are not merely quantitative, and their effects will have knock-on effects on other humans.

Perhaps most extraordinary is the way neoclassical theory, parading as "economic science" to the exclusion of all other versions of the "science" presumes that humans are innately and unalterably sociopathic, lacking in any concern for the welfare of others, except in so far as it would give them pleasure. It is worse than a Hobbesian worldview. It is the viewpoint of a religious fundamentalist who rejects the wide range of human emotions and concerns, including the notion that sharing is innate to human culture. In the neoclassical theology, we are all born sinners (or, in less religious terms, sociopaths). What is a being (homo economicus) who spends its (forget his/her) life in single-minded (blind) and unchanging pursuit of pleasure: the neoclassical vision is of the human as zombie. The lack of emotional growth means the neoclassical economic agent is the living dead. Society becomes a terrain over which these living dead feed their pleasure seeking drive.

Fortunately, humans are not zombies. Humans are dynamic and complex, ever changing .We do far more than just move from pleasure seeking consumption decision to pleasure seeking consumption decision. And starting with the assumption that this is what humans are doing will not get you much more than a good zombie novel. Even vampire movies usually have more complex living dead characters than this.

So, the only real sin is that committed by the neoclassical economists relying upon reductionism to generate policy recommendations that generate negative outcomes for the innocent: the failure to recognize institutional effects, exploitation, discrimination and other forms of exclusion, the impact of environmental damage to human health, the unfairness of wealth and income distribution (and the origins of inequalities in wealth and income distributions), the dogmatic definition of humanness as something dead and unchanging, the argument that the outcome of decisions by these zombies is the best of all possible worlds (all pardon to Voltaire) results in economic policies that deny food to the hungry, shelter to the exposed, medicine to the sick. To reiterate, we are not zombies. Humans have been changing since time immemorial and we are changing still. Perhaps eventually the neoclassical economists will change and abandon reductionism.

Each and every human being is the complex product of the diverse influences in their lives, including events uniquely experienced, friends, families, and technologies in existence at the time of her or his life. We occupy a series of unique locations in time and space. Every act we take changes others and every act of others changes us. Humanity is dynamic, in every sense. Our behavior, ideas, even biology are all constantly in flux. Reductionist notions of human beings (properly defined as bigotry) are religious fantasies (racism, for example, is nothing but a religion worshiping race, in and of itself a concept lacking any concrete, real world manifestation, as a god or, in some cases, God).

What has any of this to do with Cyberspace? Cyberspace is the arena within which a revolutionary paradigm in thinking and acting is taking place. The propaganda of the neoclassical universe is being subverted by a body of human beings acting in their collective interest to reprogram a wide range of algorithms, both those that govern the behavior of computer programs, programs that operate within a wide range of technological mediums, from servers and desktop computers to smart phones and other portable computing devices, to those algorithms that determine the functioning of societies, such as the rules for organizing groups of people to action or the modes of diffusing information within the society. The rising technomass does not care what the neoclassical theorists say, they are acting in accord with their own conception of human nature (or the lack of any such essentialism altogether—humans having no fixed nature). Cyberspace represents a spontaneous evolution of new "markets" for a wide range of use values, from applications to friendships to new forms of loans to recipes for revolutionary overthrow of dictatorial regimes. These are "markets" only in the loosest sense of the word, since the transfers occurring within Cyberspace are not necessarily exchanges but often gifts given by strangers, all bound together only by being members of the technomass, component elements in a new superorganic lifeform.

And as for another of those core theological concepts of the neoclassical paradigm, the equilibrium or equilibria, Cyberspace begins with the immediate recognition of dynamism, of disequilibria as norm. The disruptive impact of Cyberspace on all pre-existing social structures is becoming increasingly apparent, everything is being pressured to change. This is very stressful for many people, particularly those with a more conservative bent, although those with a conservative bent are always extremely selective about what they want to change and the changes they accept. The reality of Cyberspace is that it is a space that is both liberating from any norm and highly stressful for those attempting the reproduction of existing norms. Everything is subject to change in Cyberspace, from relationships of love and friendship to the way we experience travel or entertainment. And the changes experienced so far are only the beginning, since the transformations are accelerating as the technomass grows. Because every actor can impact Cyberspace (and many do so by becoming active code hackers and writers) and Cyberspace, as a digital space, is capable of extraordinary reformations in very short time spans, then change within Cyberspace is exponential.

governments need to adapt, as well. rules designed to protect boundaries, to lock the past into place, to protect monopolistic control over knowledge that is itself a product of open source, human collective invention and innovation for millennia, are barriers to fully realizing the possibilities of the new and unbounded within cyberspace, within the digital realm.

those governments that recognize the possibilities and unleash their citizenry to be entrepreneurs of the new digital/ knowledge-based/open source epoch will reap benefits in the form of economic growth and development, greater wealth and security for their citizens. those who remain locked in the fundamentalist traps will be left behind.

in the world of code and in the context of the digital, the old protest that invention requires proprietary control (protected by government enforcement) ignores or minimizes the dynamic impact of knowledge diffusion on human survival.

every successful case of economic development has been predicated on the innovation of pre-existing inventions, technology that was appropriated from the past, from blueprints and other forms of code stored within human culture. even bill shakespeare practiced open source appropriation, so did t.s. eliot, and countless others who generated the cultural foundations of "western literature." indeed, the bible is a font for stories "plagiarized" from non-Christians. so it isn't just science and commerce that appropriates. this was the way Great Britain and the U.S.A. rose, at different times, to become global superpowers. knowledge diffusion (the genetics of human culture) has always been open source.

($)

IN MOST COUNTRIES, THE CENTRAL GOVERNMENT MONOPOLIZES CONTROL OVER THE ISSUE OF CURRENCY. MONEY IS A LINK CONNECTING PEOPLE. IT ALLOWS PEOPLE TO ENGAGE IN ECONOMIC TRANSACTIONS WITHOUT THE DOUBLE COINCIDENCE REQUIRED FOR BARTER. (I WANT SOMETHING YOU HAVE. YOU HAVE SOMETHING I HAVE. IF WE CAN NEGOTIATE A TRADE THEN ALL IS GOOD.) WITH MONEY, YOU SIMPLY FIND SOMEONE WHO HAS WHAT YOU WANT AND IS WILLING TO ACCEPT MONEY, THE UNIVERSAL EQUIVALENT IN EXCHANGE. BUT WHAT IF THERE IS A SHORTAGE OF MONEY IN A COMMUNITY? THEN SOME ECONOMIC ACTIVITY WILL BE SHORT-CIRCUITED. YOU HAVE SKILLS, RESOURCES, AND CAN MAKE A PRODUCT OR PERFORM A SERVICE. THE SAME IS TRUE OF OTHERS. BUT YOU ARE ALL UNEMPLOYED BECAUSE THERE IS NOT SUFFICIENT MONEY TO GENERATE A LARGE ENOUGH LOCAL MARKET FOR YOUR (AND OTHERS') GOODS AND SERVICES. CYBERSPACE CAN BE VERY LIBERATING, BUT A LOCAL EXCHANGE TRADING SYSTEM WITH ITS OWN CURRENCY IS ALSO LIBERATING. THESE TECHNOLOGIES HAVE ONE THING IN COMMON, ELIMINATING CONSTRAINTS THAT REDUCE OUR ABILITY TO TAKE CONTROL OF OUR OWN LIVES. THEY ARE LIBERATING, BUT ONLY IF GOVERNMENT ALLOWS THEM TO BE SO.

UNFORTUNATELY, CONTROL OVER MONEY IS A CENTRAL ASPECT OF THE FUNDAMENTALIST ORDER.

SHANGHAI COMMERCIAL
JETCO
MasterCard
VISA
Cirrus
PLUS
銀联
JET PAYMENT
2520 1747

"The United States in Congress assembled shall also have the sole and exclusive right and power of regulating the alloy and value of coin struck by their own authority, or by that of the respective States — fixing the standards of weights and measures throughout the United States — regulating the trade and managing all affairs with the Indians, not members of any of the States, provided that the legislative right of any State within its own limits be not infringed or violated"

—Articles of Confederation, Article IX

OF AMERICA
B 36803124 N
WASHINGTON, D.C.
2
A 266
SERIES
1985
Secretary of the Treasury.
2
DOLLARS

CASH IS KING.

8

Fiat money, paper money, the money we are accustomed to using to meet our needs and wants, to alleviate our anxieties about the future, and to acquire the trappings of a social identity is, for all intents and purposes, a digital entity. It exists as a mathematical relationship between things, defined in terms of algorithms of exchange and laws of acquisition and possession.

Money is a social relationship, even if the underlying relationships appear invisible in its substance and use, perhaps because we have become so accustomed to money as a form of technology (which it is also) that we have lost sight of the social relationship aspect. Money is a way of controlling access to and providing for the distribution of social resources. More money gives more access, less money gives less access. Less money can also create dependence, since less access to critical resources (food, clothing, shelter, an iPod) may force one to seek a relationship with those who have more money, if that relationship solves the deficiency issue.

Money is also a form of technology (just like electricity or a hammer) that facilitates the movement of resources within society, allows for the leveraging of other types of relationships and resources, and which triggers all sorts of other processes. As a technology, money serves as a condition for the existence of a wide range of social and technological processes.

Capitalism is predicated on a system of money, where the money is controlled by centralized authorities acting to reproduce a status quo where technology is largely controlled by a small subset of the society. Capitalism cannot survive in any other environment. If money is not available, there can be no generalized exchange and labor time cannot be bought and sold on an impersonal market that reproduces the necessary illusion of equal exchange. If money is not controlled by some centralized institutional structure, whether a central bank or some other corporate body(ies), then it becomes possible for talented individuals to collaborate and create their own money, circumventing the need to engage in the renting of their bodies and minds for contracted time periods in a so-called labor market. This would undermine the very basis of capitalism, which is this renting of human bodies and minds for finite contracted periods of time.

Thus, capitalism has as one of its conditions of existence a financial/monetary system that is anti-democratic in nature. The process by which capitalism comes into being and is reproduced is one in which the vast majority of citizens must be money starved, must always need to replenish supplies of money with which to pay for necessities, to pay for social existence. Thus, capitalism requires the concentration of money.

To the extent the rising technomass provides a menas to circumvent centralized control over money, as a digital phenomena, and by diffusing the money creation process within Cyberspace to liberate exchange from the central authorities, the technomass is challenging another of the central conditions of existence of capitalism. Cybermoney is revolutionary money. Cyber loans are revolutionary loans, at least it has the potential to be so. If money can be created within he digital realm and used as medium of exchange and store of value, the bonds of a capitalist monetary system are endangered.

And if the technomass challenges capitalism, it poses a serious threat to the dominant social relationship in the society, the relationship of the human worker-machine to her/his employer.

Yet there is very little open recognition of this revolutionary aspect of the technomass. Perhaps that is all for the best. The central authorities would certainly recognize any development that explicitly challenged their monopoly control over money and might very well act decisively to nip it in the bud. Therefore, if such developments do take place as a result of the actions of the technomass, it is best that such actions happen behind the scenes, so to speak.

In the years leading to the financial crisis of 2008, large amounts of surplus capital were imported into the US from oil-driven economies in the Middle East and fast-growing economies in Asia. Housing prices were higher than ever before with no sign of going down. The inflow of capital, assisted by the proliferation of unregulated financial instruments, low interest rates, and excessive levels of leverage motivated Wall Street to supply innumerable loans to high-risk borrowers and to create a massive amount of unregulated derivative contracts based on an overly optimistic view of future housing prices.

It was no surprise that when the housing bubble finally burst a severe credit crisis emerged on Wall Street. The housing bubble had been primarily financed with debt, and many mortgages defaulted, the value of houses decreased. Derivatives linked to this debt unraveled, Wall Street neared collapse and demonstrated the financial inefficiency of this centralized system of control over money that had the power to bring the entire world economy down.

Bank of

On October 3, 2008, the Act of Congress 110-343 was signed into law by President George W. Bush. the Act created the $700 billion dollars (yes, 9 zeros) Troubled Asset Relief Program (TARP) to respond to the US financial debacle caused by the reckless creation of assets by large-scale financial firms. The money generated by these assets far exceeded the underlying value. The TARP increased the statutory limit on the public debt to US$ 11.3 trillion.

The Federal Reserve Bank is essentially the fourth wing of the US government. The Federal Reserve Bank is run by unelected officials, but has powers far in excess of those of the president of the United States to allocate money and other federal assets. The creation of TARP gave the Secretary of the Treasury Henry Paulson (former Chairman and CEO Goldman Sachs) extraordinary powers to allocate federal funds. Thus, the Fed and the Treasury became the most powerful single agencies within the federal bureaucracy, with both legislative/budgetary and executive powers, and without any direct oversight. The TARP funds were used to purchase devalued and difficult-to-value assets from financial institutions, but federal funds were also allocated to non-financial firms, such as General Motors and General Electric (both of which have financing arms but are mostly industrial firms).

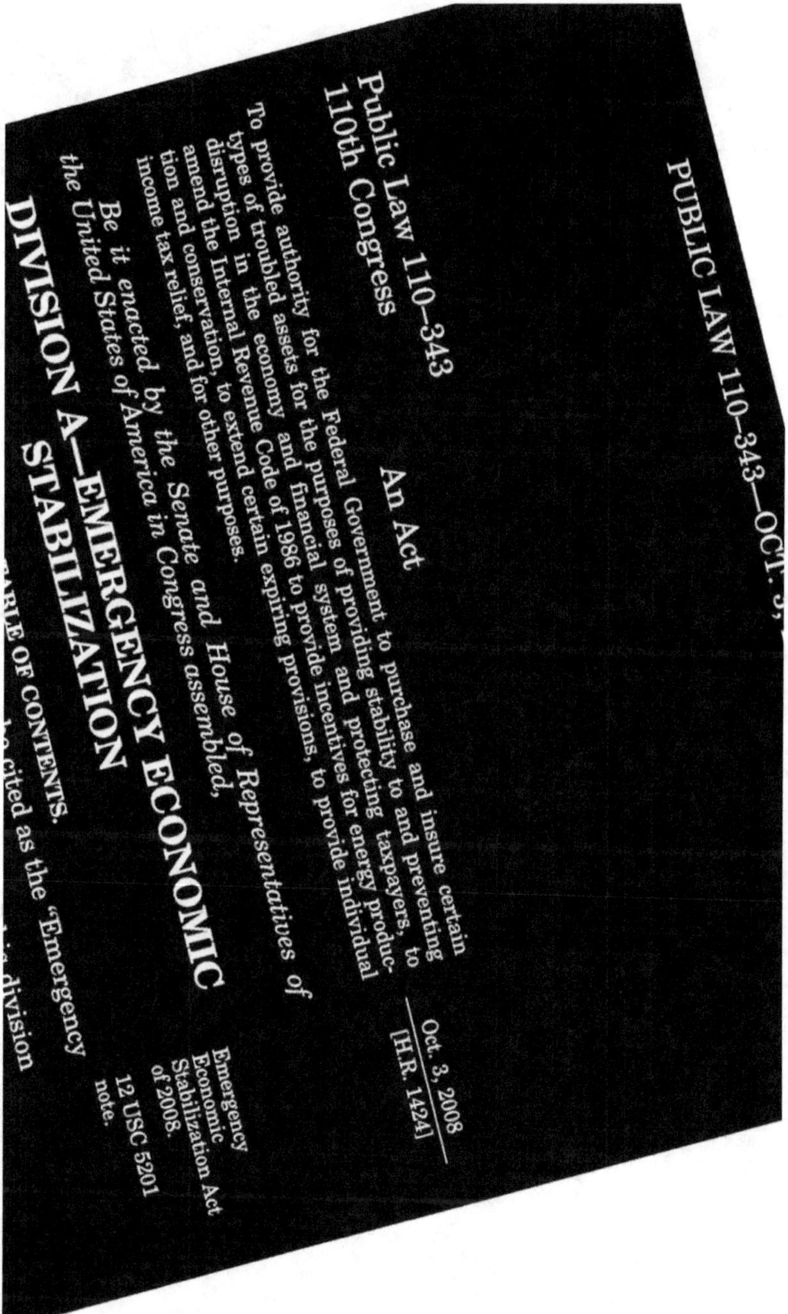

PUBLIC LAW 110–343—OCT. 3,

Public Law 110–343
110th Congress

An Act

Oct. 3, 2008
[H.R. 1424]

To provide authority for the Federal Government to purchase and insure certain types of troubled assets for the purposes of providing stability to and preventing disruption in the economy and financial system and protecting taxpayers, to amend the Internal Revenue Code of 1986 to provide incentives for energy production and conservation, to extend certain expiring provisions, to provide individual income tax relief, and for other purposes.

Be it enacted by the Senate and House of Representatives of the United States of America in Congress assembled,

Emergency Economic Stabilization Act of 2008.

12 USC 5201 note.

DIVISION A—EMERGENCY ECONOMIC STABILIZATION

ABLE OF CONTENTS.

cited as the "Emergency

division

The federal authorities failed to regulate the way Wall Street firms created new financial derivatives, including exotic insurance contracts, that were grounded on faith, not probability.

Alan Greenspan was treated as a guru of economics. Yet the contemporary global economy of corporate structures, derivative contracts, outsourced and off-shored exploitation, and rapid technological change is beyond the limits of the current state of the art in economic theory to explain, much less manage.

G: "I have found a flaw. I don't know how significant or permanent it is. But I have been very distressed by that fact."

W: "In other words, you found that your view of the world, your ideology, was not right, it was not working"

G: "You know, that's precisely the reason I was shocked, because I have been going for 40 years or more with very considerable evidence that it was working exceptionally well."

Congressional testimony October 23, 2008 G: Alan Greenspan and W: Henry Waxman

we the state

"...HAVE DECIDED,
THAT THE FEW, THE
TOO BIG
AND TOO
IMPORTANT
TO FAIL,
HAVE REGAINED THE
PRIVILEGE TO CONTINUE
OPERATIONS,
ALTHOUGH THEIR
SERVICE TO OUR
SOCIETY HAS BECOME
OBSOLETE"

the obsolete

we fight because we must survive. we fight because we are threatened. we fight because we fear. we fight because our lord protects us. we fight because we fight. we fight because we already know that we are already dead

war

9

Obsolete War

We are in the midst of a new kind of war; a war with no M4 carbine, no H6 bombs, and no soldiers in uniform. This is a war of codes. This is a war over the diffusion of knowledge. It is a war in which emerging open codes are replacing the established closed codes and where tightly controlled knowledge transfer is being replaced by widespread, unfiltered, uncensored diffusion of knowledge by the technomass. Whether Wikipedia or Wikileaks, the technomass has been intervening in the diffusion of all forms of knowledge. A mass of code writers has been similarly intervening in the very mechanisms by which technology operates, including the technologies driving Cyberspace itself.

These code wars pose a challenge to the centralized-command-bureaucratic institutions that have dominated social life in most of the world, acting as a form of imperialist force shaping work, play, and identity. The centralized-command-bureaucratic institutions are being replaced by open source-commons-based heterogeneous movements. Thus, work, play, and identity are being transformed. Capitalist society had created an environment where more and more of an individual's life was mediated by corporate structures and/or a corporate-dominated governmental bureaucracy. The technologies and social relationships that have given rise to Cyberspace have broken through this mediation process and allowed direct connections to be formed between individuals—forming the technomass. Cultural, economic, and political structures formed by closed codes for the past two centuries are eroding, being replaced by new more open structures. Closed codes have been a key factor to maintaining a pyramid-like social structure, providing the means for corporate and governmental structures to control individual lives in sometimes subtle and sometimes not so subtle ways. The illusion of freedom came in the form of individual's selecting from a corporate and governmental predetermined choice set: you could buy a red Ford or a blue Honda, for example. You could work at IBM or you could work at Microsoft or you could work at Apple. However open codes are undermining the traditional social order. and it is becoming increasingly easy to work for yourself, to detach from the corporate structures and subvert the governmental bureaucracy. The transformation is hardly complete, but it clearly continuing in a wide variety of ways, pushed forward by a rising technomass, occurring within the expanding Cyberspace. Open codes are providing the conditions for new social systems that do not require top-down organizations to properly function and thrive. A new kind of citizen is being assembled by open codes. Individuals are becoming non geo-bounded entrepreneurial citizens of the Technomass. And the information flows within the this technomass are increasingly independent of centralized authorities.

Centralized authorities will not go quietly into that good night of late capitalism. Big banks, megacorporations, and governments are struggling to maintain their dominion in a world where a rapidly growing and decentralizing technomass is becoming more and more pervasive in people's lives. As open codes are reshaping old paradigms and establishing new forms of economic and social exchange, corporate structures are sometimes turning to the government, either through regulatory authority or judicial action, to protect their imperialistic position within social life. Intellectual property rights have been expanded, both in terms of the number of social technics covered and the temporal lifespan of existing rihts over old technics. A widescale propaganda campaign has been waged to convince individuals of the inalienable rights of corporate structures to own this wider span of social technics, even convincing some people that their own DNA shoud be patentable by corporate entities. Nevertheless, the technomass resists. Individuals within Cyberspace are increasingly behaving as sovereign units rather than citizens of sovereign states. The free and unregulated access to digital means of production is channeling a fundamentally new form of human development and creating new conditions for liberation. At the same time, information dissemination is shattering the monopoly of corporate media over the "news," with most people under 25 years of age now getting most of their news from the technomass.

Centralized-command-bureaucratic entities will go to war and try to stop the emerging open codes and open knowledge diffusion *by any means necessary*. However, if any corporate-government force wins, they risk making their society obsolete. This is the irony of Cyberspace, which transcends national borders. To win at blocking the increasing freedom allowed within Cyberspace is to cripple one society in the race to advance the technological and social boundaries made possible by Cyberspace. Any country that blocks its citizens participation in the technomass, only blocks the diffusion of knowledge within that society, granting competitive advantages to other societies. The odds of a global concord to block the advance of the technomass is unlikely. Therefore, the war of the centralized authorities against the rising technomass is already obsolete.

"The validity of the public debt of the United States, authorized by law, including debts incurred for payment of pensions and bounties for services in suppressing insurrection or rebellion, shall not be questioned."

—Fourteenth Amendment
to the United States Constitution,
Section IV

central

mass

"let us sin then, and sin to infinity"

—Michel Foucault

Sin is a side effect of centralized power. Authorities who sought to control the behavior of "the masses" recognized the efficiency of controlling the definition of Truth and Justice and of gaining access to the inner motivations of individuals by programming them to short-circuit certain behaviors and so sin was born. The decentralized Technomass has begun to generate its own "morality," democratize access to the divine, and to challenge the behavioral restrictions that reproduced privilege and elite power.

open source and communications technology opens an entire new dimension of economic and political possibilities. centralized entities have dominated the globe for a long time, but now this is history. this is the age of the liberation.

March 1978, Security, Population, Territory: Lectures at the Collège de France, 2007, Michel Senellart, trans. Graham Burchell

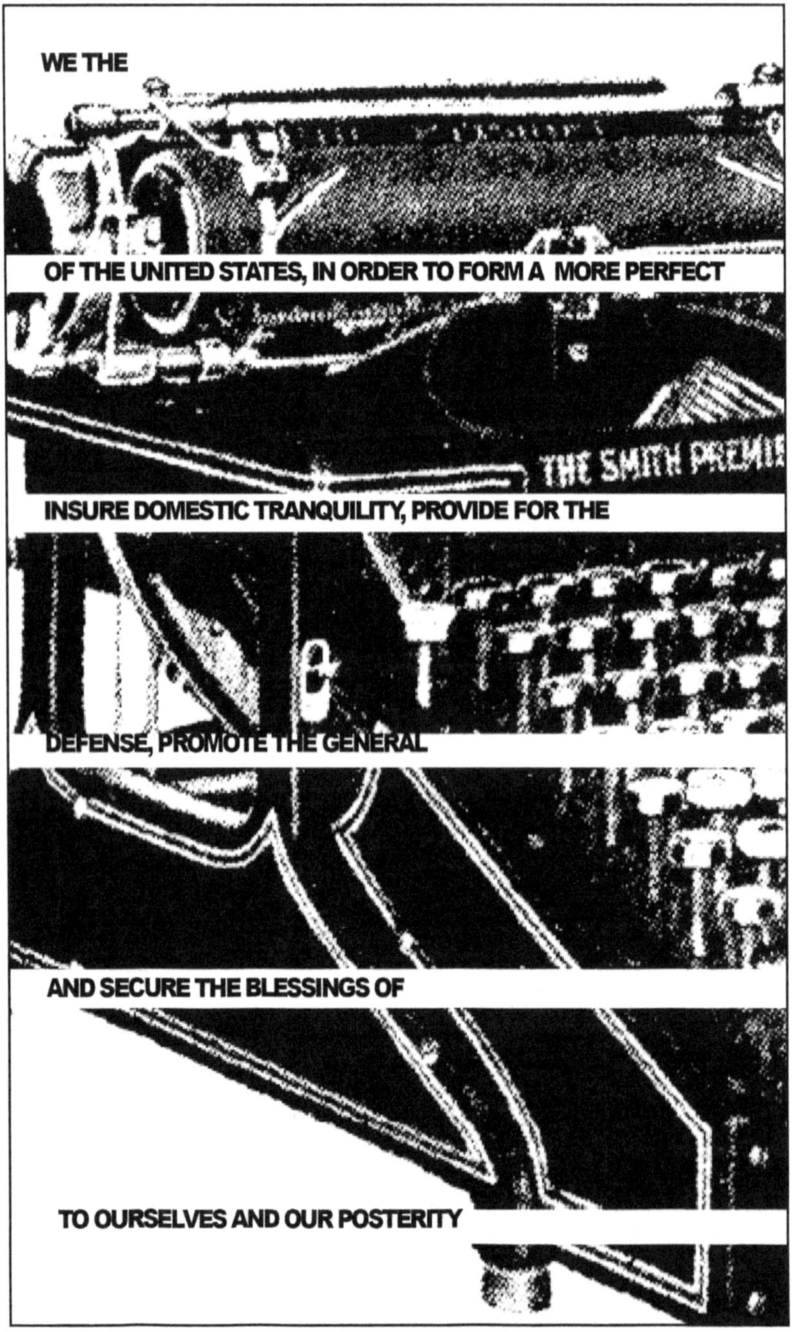
WE THE
OF THE UNITED STATES, IN ORDER TO FORM A MORE PERFECT
THE SMITH
INSURE DOMESTIC TRANQUILITY, PROVIDE FOR THE
DEFENSE, PROMOTE THE GENERAL
AND SECURE THE BLESSINGS OF
TO OURSELVES AND OUR POSTERITY

PEOPLE
UNION, ESTABLISH
JUSTICE,
TYPEWRITER
COMMON
WELFARE,
LIBERTY
№10
DO ORDAIN AND ESTABLISH THIS CONSTITUTION FOR THE
UNITED STATES OF
AMERICA

I looked out the window;

Joel whispered from behind:

“my friend, revolution”

revolution? what kind of revolution? —I asked

I looked out the window again ...

INDEED, REVOLUTION ....

Eug Delacroix
1830.

TO UNDERSTAND THE CONCEPT,

YOU SHOULD THINK OF FREE AS IN FREE SPEECH, NOT AS IN FREE BEER

10

As Althusser might have said, the Technomass is a process without a subject. This is not to imply that the countless individuals who comprise the technomasses are not catalysts behind it's evolutionary path, but that each and every one of us is part of something larger, each of us driven, in part, by the Technomass itself and the extraordinary possibilities embodied in constantly metamorphosizing code, by endless invention and innovation driven by the requirements of creating a living, superorganic force that is changing the way we live, the way we transact, the way we share, the way we learn, the way we teach, the way we think of the world we live in, the way we work, the way work environments are structured and restructured, the way we love and are loved, and the relationships between us and the institutions we have created to supply the requirements of life, whether governments or corporate institutions, industrial or financial firms.

Modes of production, modes of life are complex combinations of social relationships and the artifacts of technology, where the social relationships are, in fact, just another form of technology. Thus, the changes generated by the rising Technomass are not simply the product of technological innovation but are, in fact, directly generative of technology, in both hard and soft forms. It is possible to think of human beings as simply another part of this technological gestalt, also changing, also in flux. The core of human-ness remains, as Marx defined it, the "species-being," the creative urge that drives human innovation, love, life itself. The Technomass is driven, in part, by this "species-being" but it is also influenced by other social forces, products of a society that has been shaped by generations of exploitative relationships and power hierarchies, abuse and oppression. This complex gestalt is the Technomass, containing the potential for liberation and the potential to be subverted and redirected away from liberation. This struggle is economic, political, and cultural. It is also biological, because the Technomass is superorganic.

Thus, exploitation and alienation will not disappear because of the technomass. Perhaps it contains the potentiality for liberation, for the ending of a wide range of oppressions/abuse, including exploitation, but even if this potential is realized, it will not happen right away. This is not some sort of instant revolutionary soup that makes everything okay all at once or even within a day. Indeed, one should anticipate that the structures of oppression and exploitation may be reproduced in new and creative ways by tapping into the Technomass, by manipulating the thoughts and dreams of the technomasses no less than the uninitiated hordes who do not understand technology but simply sit in awe of the digital high-definition images streaming into their eyes (being simply programmed, rather than a programmer). We will see the new technological wonders of our age deployed to squeeze even more surplus value out of clueless drones who are not much different from the battery-people of *The Matrix*, each hooked up to the new technological tools in order to better order their work, rather than to connect them to a technomass within which they might find their own voice and break free like Neo to find the power in their own talents and creativity, liberated forever from "The Matrix".

In other words, take nothing for granted. The birth of the Technomass does not guarantee the life of the Technomasses or the future.... Indeed, the worse thing one can do is think the future is guaranteed. The future is uncertain and being shaped every day by our actions and inactions and by the bureaucrats in the corporate and government offices.

Nothing is guaranteed, except that nothing is guaranteed. If you want to make a better world, to realize the liberating potential in the Technomass, then it is up to you to do something about it, to join the struggle, to fight for the political freedom of open source, the freedom of collective action, the collective right to view and modify code, to remix the artifacts of the past to create something new.

Code has always played a critical role in human history: code in the form of language, blueprints, maps, music, even our DNA. Open source code has been the norm. Whether it is our fairy tales, our songs, our machines, or sex, code has been widely available and very liberally shared, creating the humanity that we have been and are. Today it is possible to take patents out on life itself. This process of placing boundaries around the most precious forms of code threatens this history of sharing. The ideology of denying access to code, of punishing the alteration of code, the remixing of code is something relatively new and the implications only barely understood. It reinforces existing asymmetries of power and threatens to short-circuit far more innovation and invention than it might foster. The Technomass has, to a large extent, been difficult to control and forms a bio-technological obstacle to the development of closed systems of control over code. It is far too easy to rebel against these systems within the Technomass, which is constantly integrating code in a manner that allows for radically creative responses to all attempts at such control. The Technomass is constituted, in part, by a radical revisioning of society and social relationships that does not accept control as the predicate for life. Thus, the idea of liberation is not radical within the Technomass.

copy+multiply
copy+multiply
copy+multiply
copy+multiply
copy+multiply
copy+multiply
copy+multiply
copy+multiply
copy+multiply

free/libre and open source technologies empower humanity's creative and innovative nature by enhancing our liberty to produce decentralized social configurations

copy+multiply

"who gets to control technology is a question that directly affects every user, whether they know it or not. when people have control over their technologies they become empowered to achieve whatever they intend to achieve"

—Benjamin Mako Hill

(A)

free and open source codes employ metamorphic capabilities that yield innovations

(T)

this feature allows the assemblage of generative interrelations in political, economic, and social realms

(G)

such elemental source codes constitute the power of decentralized technomasses

(C)

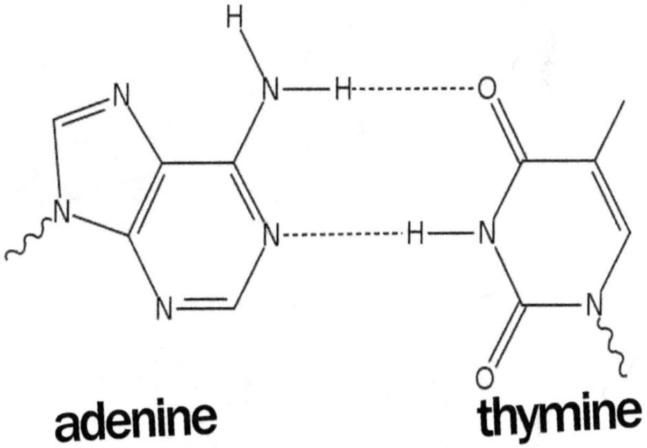
H
N
H
O
N
N
N
H
N
N
N
O
adenine
thymine

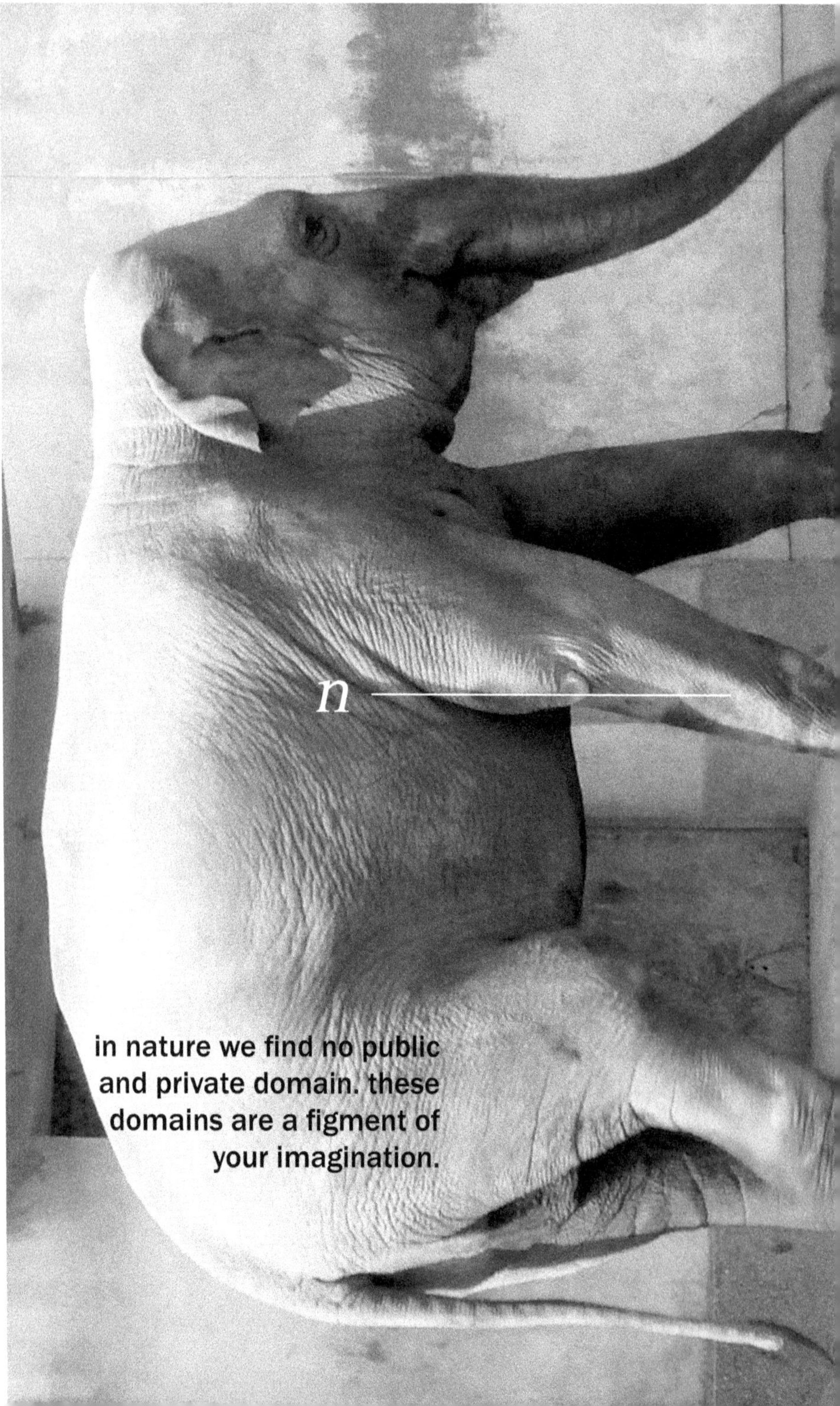

n

in nature we find no public and private domain. these domains are a figment of your imagination.

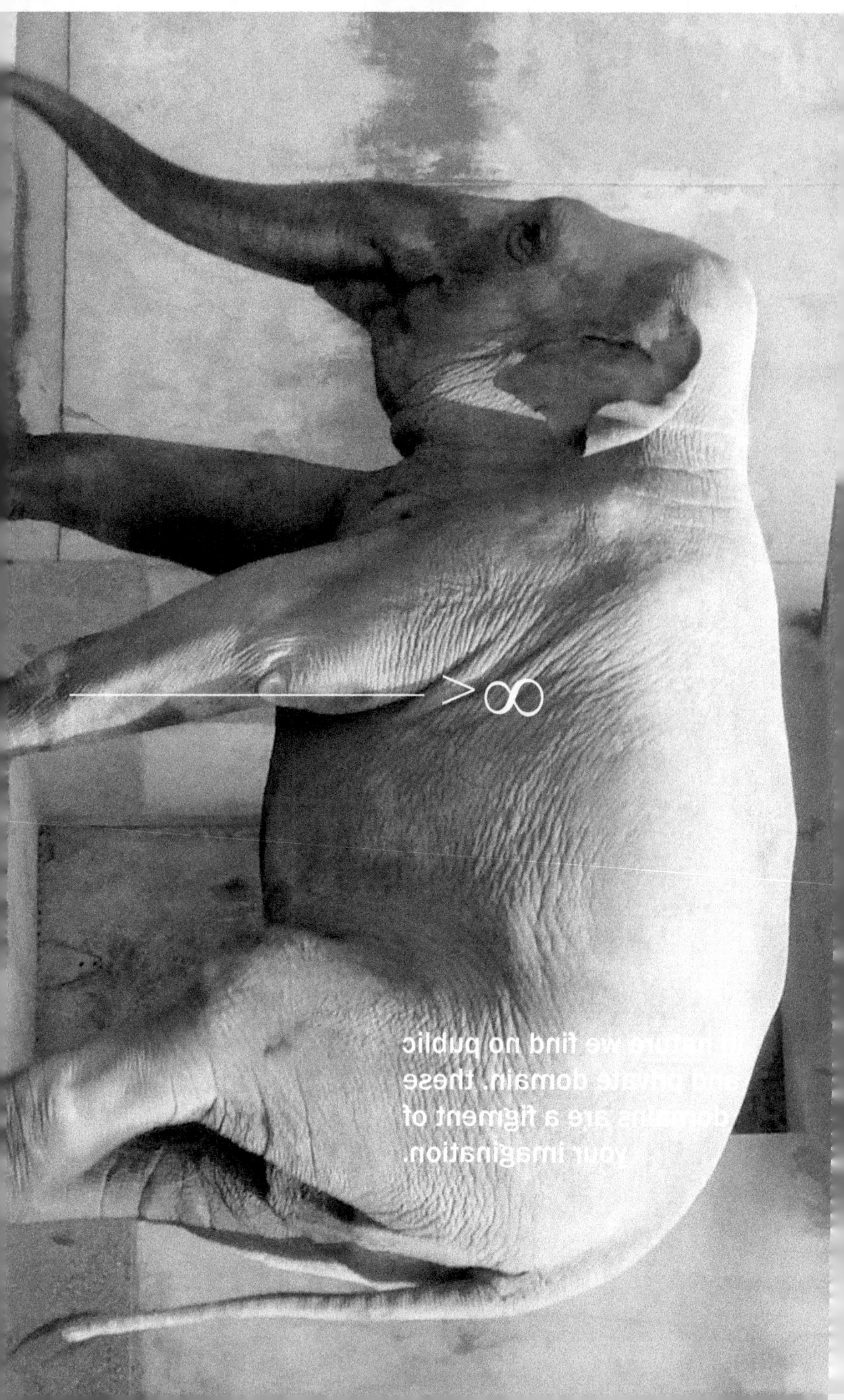
we find no public
domain. these
are a figment of
your imagination.

Wealth

The process of multiplying wealth and who benefits from the multiplied wealth, is a question of what is the dominant force driving social production. Human beings are innately social. Production is but one manifestation of our social nature. However, throughout history the multiplication of wealth has been strictly controlled and regulated by centralized entities commanding social production (the minds and talents of collectives of individual homo sapiens). Religions controlled wealth in the name of gods or God; kings have controlled wealth in the name of natural rights (linked to a notion of transcendental birth rights and the innate (read racial) superiority of those of divine

11

birth); corporations controlled wealth in the name of legally constituted rights of a superorganic subject (often bestowed with greater rights than ordinary citizens) and nations controlled wealth in the name of sovereignty. All these social configurations have been based on assigning particular entities the power to own, manage, and profit from the multiplication of wealth created by individual homo sapiens whose work takes place under the supervision and, often, coercion of an institutional structure outside of their control. Of course whenever these individual homo sapiens (non-ruling parties) have questioned the norm of social production, centralized entities have applied the right to exclusion and sometimes legalized violence to stop any disruptive activities—all this violence in the name of gods, nature, sovereignty.

These command and control systems have costs. Human creativity is stifled in many instances. Some human talents are completely rejected by the dominant structures and left to be unemployed or underemployed, denied access to technology or the community of other human beings with whom they might collaborate to generate innovations and new forms of wealth. By tightly controlling social production, centralized entities are able to control the distribution of wealth within the society and those who align themselves to the structure can benefit with larger shares of that wealth. However, this is simply another form of waste, as these managers and sycophants for the status quo consume wealth without generating innovation or new wealth, but simply engage in practices designed to reproduce the centralized power and the command and control structure.

Social production effectively increases when generative technologies are employed by individuals to multiply tangible and non-tangible wealth at very low costs. To paraphrase Althusser, closed source and related laws are the legal expressions of a closed social structure. Wide availability of knowledge facilitates the conditions for the wide availability (democratization) of social wealth. These conditions empower individuals to operate as the main driving agents behind the cultural, economic, and political spheres.

This has long been an important aspect of the academic world, where open source is manifest in a number of ways, including the practice of publishing papers in academic journals as a route to academic success. Academics are encouraged to share knowledge, to glean ideas and research data from colleagues and then remix this knowledge in innovative ways in their own papers and books, providing proper attribution for the sources of their raw material and thereby showing respect for the talents and hard work of those colleagues. However, it is always understood that the academic project is a collective and open source project. The capitalist modality that has pervaded all aspects of social life certainly has had some effect within academia. It is not unusual for a subset of academics to join in the rush for commodification of ideas and the celebration of intellectual property rights as a means for individual enrichment. And certainly there have been some strains in the open source academic model as centralized governmental entities have often found ways to exploit academics for their own objectives. More recently corporate entities from outside the academic sphere have become dissatisfied with waiting for innovations to be published in the open source journals and then gleaning exploitable knowledge from these sources. Some of these for-profit corporate structures have tried to develop direct social links to not-for-profit academic institutions or individual academics that would allow for the direct exploitation of the extraordinary talent of intellectuals who are otherwise tied by salary and commitments solely to the academic institutions. Since the rise of liberal economic ideology in the 1980s, the push for academic institutions to become more closed source and commercial in focus has been relentless. Centralized government and the command and control corporate structures have joined forces to reshape academic relationships, cash flows, and commitments. Governments direct funding to academic institutions in ways that influence policy changes toward more closed source research and closer linkages to for-profit corporate structures. These relationships are often described as "partnerships," as if the academic institutions were something more than knowledge farms to be harvested by the centralized entities. Indeed, even universities whose faculty and administrators had traditionally avoided direct links to profit-oriented enterprise structures have been pulled into the closed source game of attempting to construct legal boundaries around knowledge and control intellectual property rights, although the tension between the open source traditions and the borrowed closed source traditions of non-academic command and control structures appears in numerous ways on campuses.

The closed source model ultimately depends upon the command and control system that has not been very popular among academics. Centralized entities control and regulate social production through appropriation, violence (or the threat thereof), and fear. The power of these entities is legitimized by the violence they imposed over the ruled, and the sustained fear they ingrained. Academics have, on the other hand, relied more heavily on the cultural processes of persuasion and reward systems based on demonstrating one's ability to meet the expectations (open source) of peers. Times are changing. The coercion of governments defending particular cultural, economic, and social interests (who find it convenient to have the state do their dirty work) is becoming obsolete. Technological innovations have given individuals access to the same knowledge and resources as centralized entities. This level playing field fundamentally redefines the social relation between the ruler and the ruled. The Technomass has become connected to a powerful and transformative knowledge pool. Thus, the ruler's position has become vulnerable; the individual is being empowered.

In the decentralized Technomass, individuals

are driving the multiplication of knowledge *and* the creation of new forms of wealth.

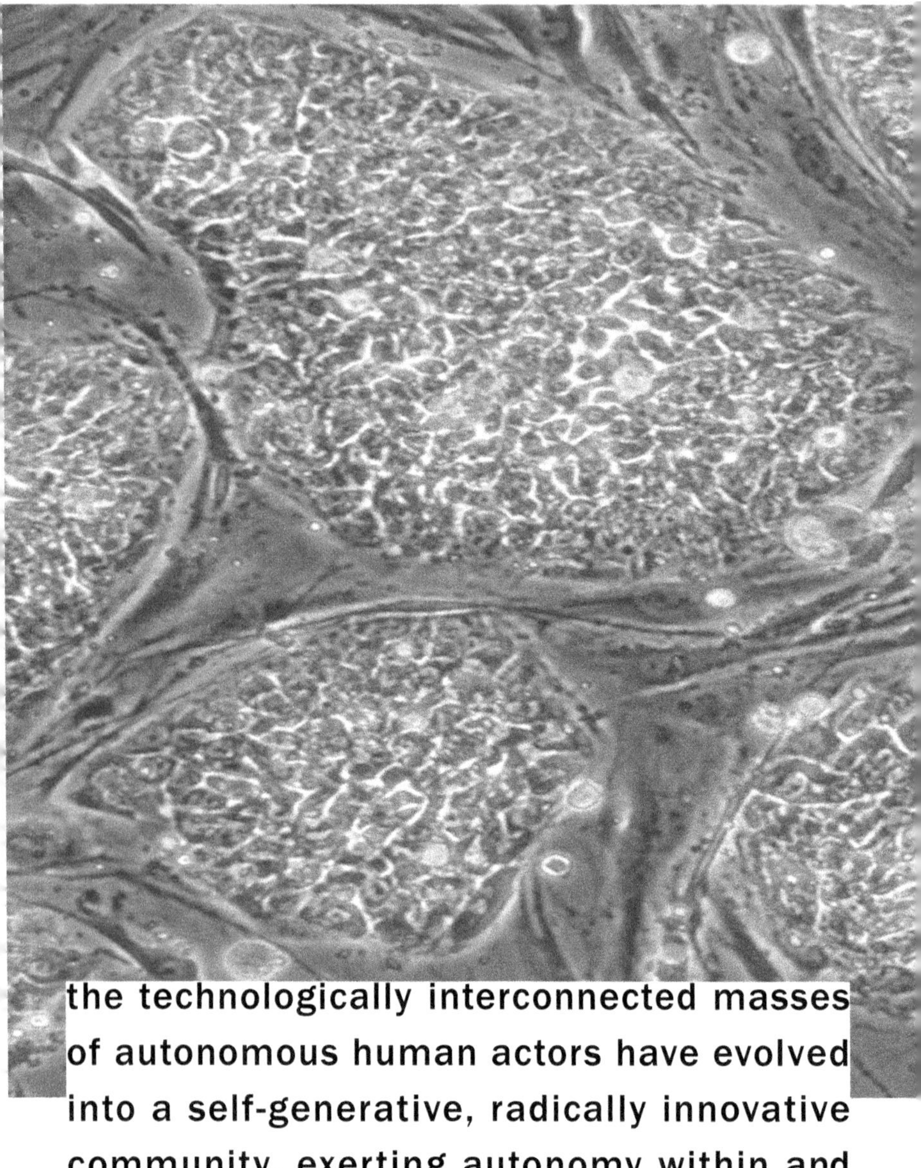

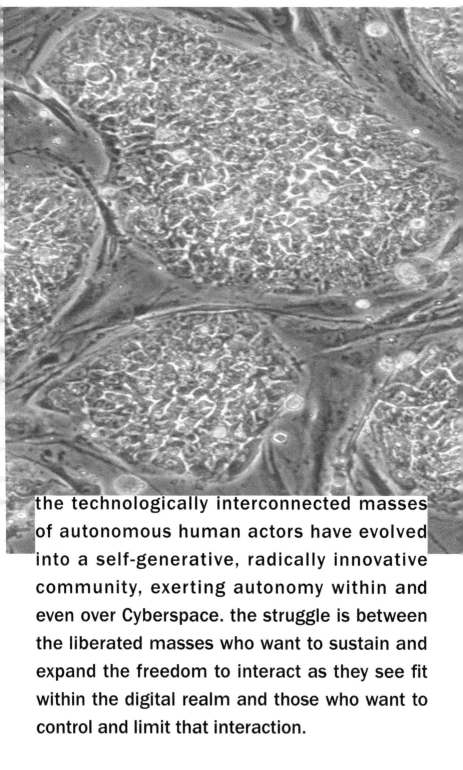

the technologically interconnected masses of autonomous human actors have evolved into a self-generative, radically innovative community, exerting autonomy within and even over Cyberspace. the struggle is between the liberated masses who want to sustain and expand the freedom to interact as they see fit within the digital realm and those who want to control and limit that interaction.

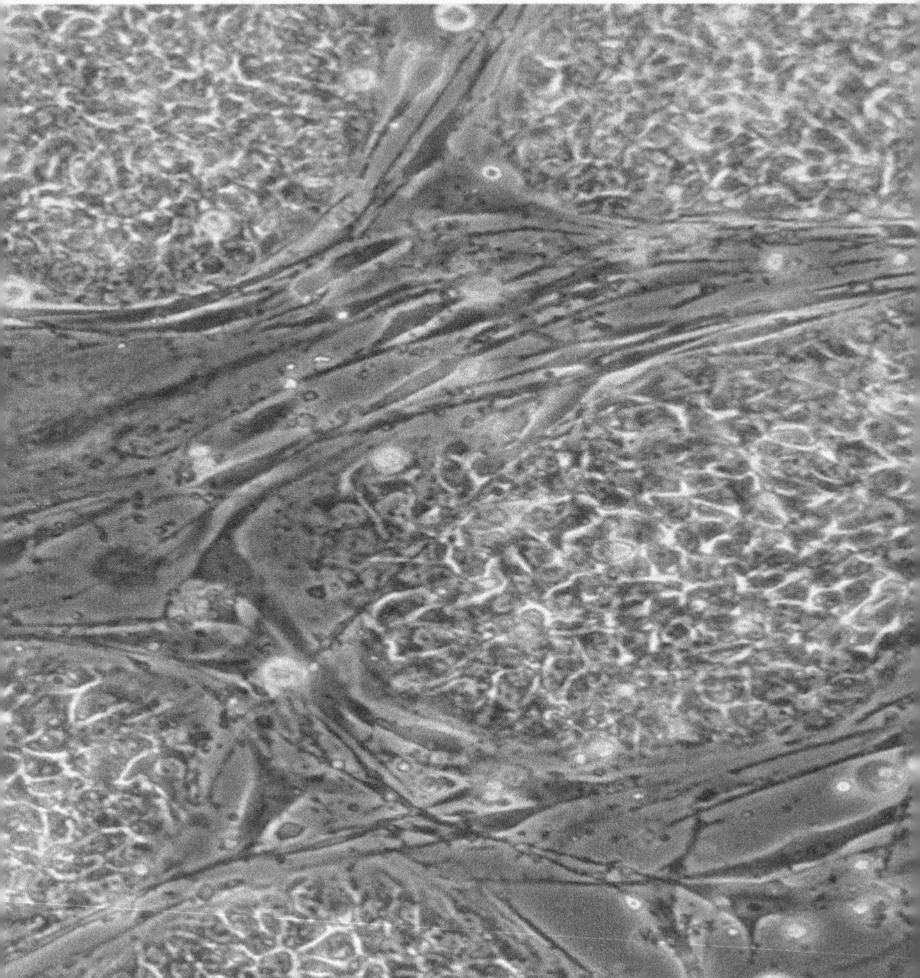

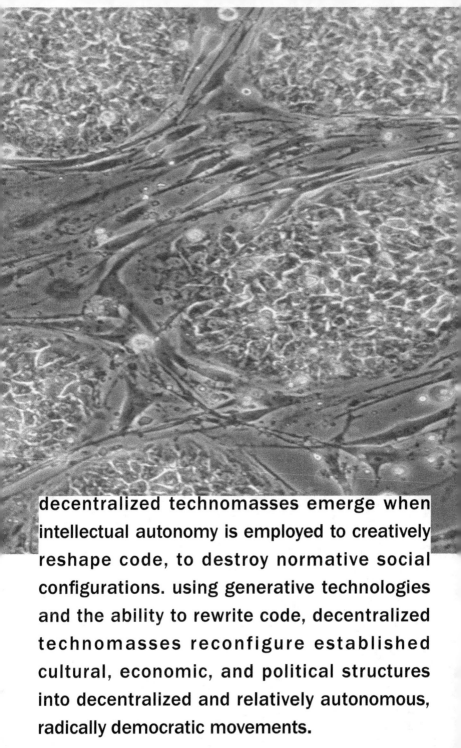

decentralized technomasses emerge when intellectual autonomy is employed to creatively reshape code, to destroy normative social configurations. using generative technologies and the ability to rewrite code, decentralized technomasses reconfigure established cultural, economic, and political structures into decentralized and relatively autonomous, radically democratic movements.

The theoretical problematic of the old regime was based on a barren concept of controlling human agency and the fruits of that agency.

Althusser understood that the old "problematic" would produce the seeds for the rise of a new society. Indeed, it was a "problematic" because it posed problems in need of solution: the rising Technomass is that solution.

NO. 31
—JACKSON POLLOCK

(we share because we must survive. we share because we
can. we share because we are not afraid. we share because
we serve no lord. we share because we share. we share
because we already know that sharing is the way to go.)

"I THINK THEY (THE PUBLIC) SHOULD NOT LOOK FOR, BUT LOOK PASSIVELY — AND TRY TO RECEIVE WHAT THE PAINTING HAS TO OFFER AND NOT BRING A SUBJECT MATTER OR PRECONCEIVED IDEA OF WHAT THEY ARE TO BE LOOKING FOR"

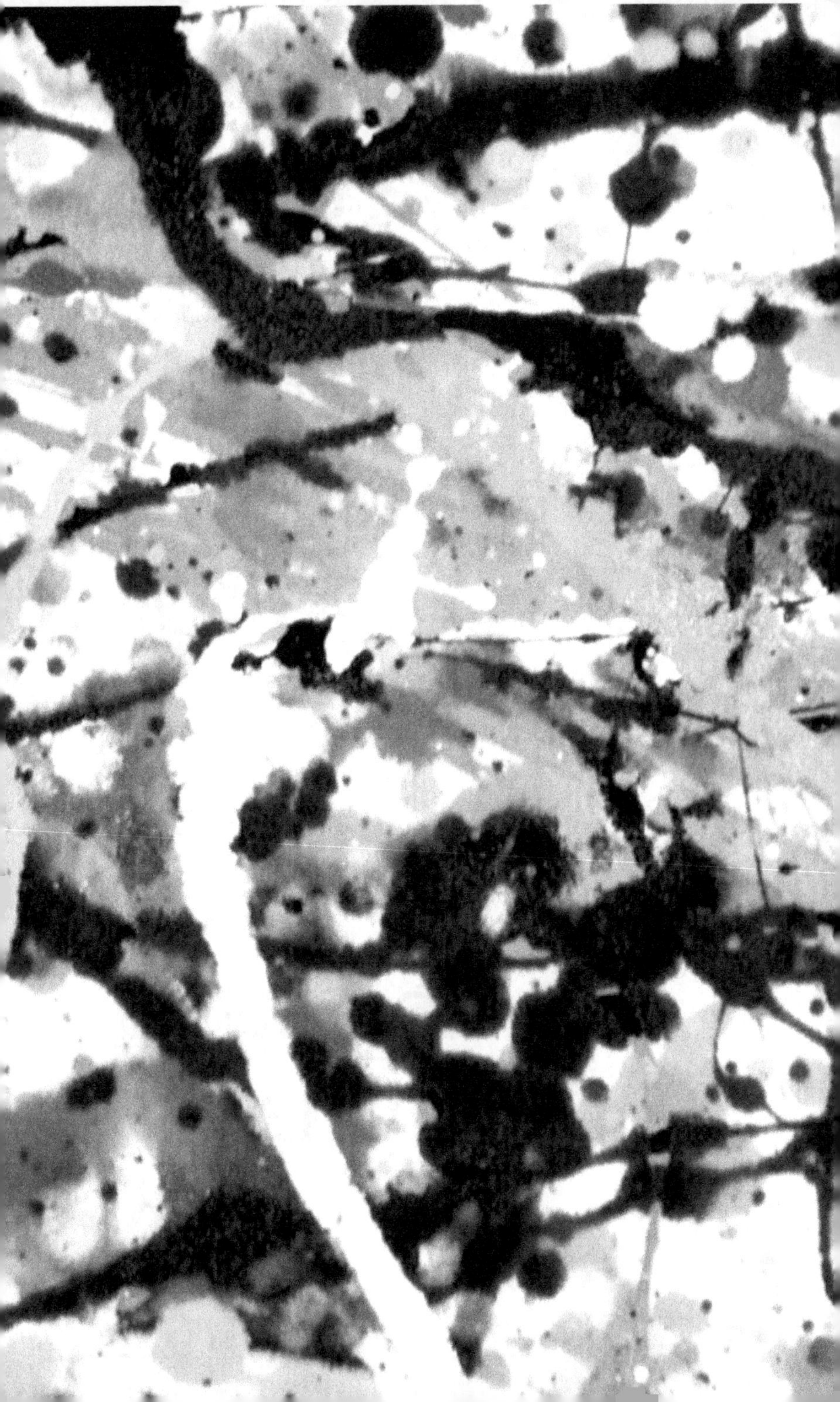

has anyone
ever told you
that
change
always comes
within
the
source ?
—i guess
this is a good
time for a
story

GRAPHY
WRITING
GEO
EARTH
GRAFIA
ESCRIBIR
GEO
TIERRA

as decentralized technomasses emerge the lines crafted by centralized entities to bound geo-citizens begin to vanish.

soon we realize that we are all one interdependent mass. freedom of digital locomotion brings about synergistic configurations that facilitate proper conditions for the multiplication of generative endeavors. we are, indeed, all brothers and sisters. we're in this together.

for centuries centralized entities have monopolized official education. students have been primarily trained to serve the needs of an aristocracy (whether feudal, slave, or capitalist), and thus education has focused on a particular set of intellectual abilities. for those individuals who did not fit the mold there haven't been many alternatives.

—the fundamental theoretical basis for the status quo is the Platonic belief that innate abilities define one's position in the social order. The decentralized, radically democratic Technomass poses a challenge to this reactionary ideology.

EXIT

EDUCATION IS RADICALLY TRANSFORMED BY TECHNOMASSES. DECENTRALIZED EDUCATIONAL MOVEMENTS AND A DO IT YOURSELF ETHIC, POWERED BY GENERATIVE TECHNOLOGIES, ALLOWS INDIVIDUALS TO FREELY LEARN MORE THAN EVER BEFORE. THIS RESULTS IN A SOCIAL MIX IN WHICH MORE INDIVIDUALS HAVE ACCESS TO THE INTELLECTUAL MEANS TO BECOME AUTONOMOUS. TECHNOMASSES REASSEMBLE THE PROCESS OF EDUCATION BY BRINGING FREE AND OPEN KNOWLEDGE TO THE MASSES.

once we have knowledge,

the story can be something else

How to Connect to a Sending and Receiving Infrastructure

cyberspace redefines who, how, what, and where we communicate. traditional one-way mediums only engage with users as consumers. as a result, the quality, quantity, and distributions of knowledge only vary based on how much content users are willing to consume. in economic terms, the barriers of entry to traditional one-way mediums are so high that individual users are unlikely to participate. cyberspace transforms this situation. the production and distribution of knowledge greatly increases by dramatically lowering the barriers of entry, linking users and producers from around the globe in a multi-way medium, and creating a wide array of decentralized networks. cyberspace empowers individuals by allowing access to more knowledge in more places.

when knowledge is democratized individuals have more opportunities to shape their environments. cultural, economic, and political structures are shaped to the particular needs of a given technomass. this renders societies assembled by the power of innovation.

How to Make Your Own Television Receiver

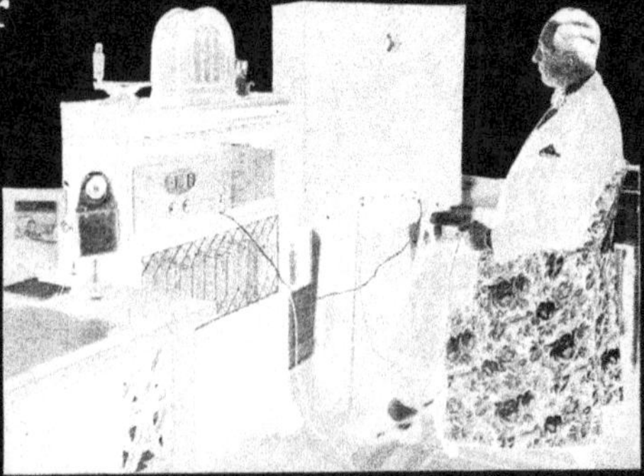

H. Gernsback, Editor of Radio News, receiving the television broadcasts from WRNY at his home in New York City, with the simple apparatus described in this article. For purposes of the test, the neon tube and loud speaker were connected in series temporarily, with successful operation simultaneously.

IN order to pick up and reproduce the television images now being broadcast by WRNY and W2XAL, you need only a modest assembly of instruments, some of which you probably already have on hand, and some of which you will have to buy.

First, since the television images are transmitted simultaneously on 326 and 30.91 meters, by WRNY and W2XAL, respectively, you need either a regular broadcast tuner or a short-wave tuner. If you live in or near New York, and obtain satisfactory loud-speaker results from the regular WRNY transmissions, all you require is a separate audio-amplifier of the resistance-coupled type, and the scanning mechanism, to be described later. If you are already using a resistance-coupled amplifier, as many radio fans are, you will need only the scanning apparatus.

If you cannot hear WRNY's 326-meter wave very well, the best thing to do is to install a short-wave set, in order to pick up the 30.91-meter wave of W2XAL. You will require the audio amplifier also, however. Happily, short-wave receivers are very inexpensive and can be built very easily, so you should assemble one without delay. It will enable you to pick up, not only W2XAL's television signals, but also the "radio-movies" of station 3XK (using the Jenkins system), and musical programs from short-wave broadcast stations in many parts of the world. We can particularly recommend the set described in the Radio News Free Blueprint No. 62. This uses an R.F. amplifying stage, has only one tuning control, and costs very little to assemble. If you do not already own a short-wave receiver, just drop us a card and we will send you Blueprint No. 62 free of charge.

In making this receiver, do not install the single stage of audio amplification. Leave out the audio transformer and the third tube, and simply provide two binding posts for the wires that are shown connected to the primary posts of this transformer. The detector is then easily connected to an external resistance-coupled audio amplifier.

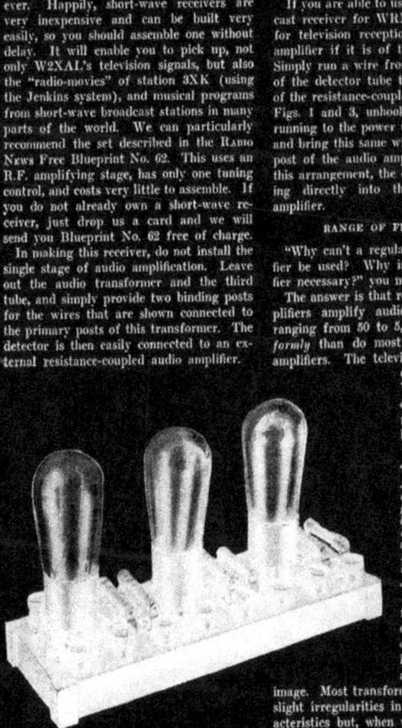

A commercial three-stage amplifier which may be purchased already assembled is convenient and compact. The 171-type tube in the output is best suited to the characteristics of the neon tube.

If you are able to use your regular broadcast receiver for WRNY, you will not use for television reception the present audio amplifier if it is of the transformer type. Simply run a wire from the plate (P) post of the detector tube to the top input post of the resistance-coupled amplifier shown in Figs. 1 and 3, unhook the "B+Det" wire running to the power unit or "B" batteries, and bring this same wire to the other input post of the audio amplifier instead. With this arrangement, the detector will be feeding directly into the resistance-coupled amplifier.

RANGE OF FREQUENCIES

"Why can't a regular transformer amplifier be used? Why is a resistance amplifier necessary?" you may ask.

The answer is that resistance-coupled amplifiers amplify audio-frequency impulses ranging from 50 to 5,000 cycles *more uniformly* than do most transformer-coupled amplifiers. The television impulses broadcast by WRNY-W2XAL and others cover this frequency range, and they must be reproduced faithfully at the receiving end, without emphasis on any particular register, in order to create a recognizable image. Most transformer amplifiers possess slight irregularities in their response characteristics but, when voice or music is being reproduced, these are not very noticeable to the ear. When television images are being reproduced, even the slightest irregularity will cause the already crude images to break up and assume peculiar shapes. The general experience of television experimenters has been that resistance-coupled amplifiers are more satisfactory for both television transmitters and receivers, at least in this stage of the art.

The above statements should not be interpreted as a condemnation of the transformer amplifier. There has long been raging in technical circles a controversy over the respective merits of the transformer and resistance systems for the amplification of voice and musical signals, with the radio experts evenly divided between the two camps. At the present time, however, it is easier to get good pictures from the latter system, so we recommend resistance coupling. However, it is entirely possible to obtain satisfactory results from a *high-quality* transformer arrangement; witness the work being done by James Millen, of Malden, Mass., whose experiments are described briefly on page 421 of this issue.

A good three-stage resistance-coupled amplifier can easily be assembled on a wooden board, about five inches wide and twelve inches long. A completely-assembled one can be bought for about ten dollars, but a home-made one will not cost so much. After you finish it, you will have a fine amplifier, not only for television impulses, but for regular broadcast programs as well.

DESIGN OF AN AMPLIFIER

You will need the following parts, arranged and connected as shown in Figs. 1 and 3: a wooden baseboard; three UX-type tube sockets, V1, V2, V3; three ¼-ampere filament ballast resistors, R4; two double-resistor mountings; four 0.5-mf. fixed condensers of the by-pass type, C; one 1.0-mf. condenser, C1; a special high-value grid

individuals empowered by generative technologies have the tools to shape their environments locally, and to globally empower others. technomasses transform ordinary citizens into autonomic agents. these agents are the main innovation drivers worldwide.

global citizenship

local
technomasses
global citizenship assembles
social configurations in which individuals
have the freedom to be self-determined.

WHEN CENTRALIZED ENTITIES START THINKING ABOUT TECHNOMASSES:

"MASSIVE

CHANGES IN TECHNOLOGIES MAKE POSSIBLE THE LINKING OF PEOPLE ACROSS THE WORLD"

"THERE IS A HUGE OPPORTUNITY OPENING TO US THAT HAS NEVER [BEEN] OPEN BEFORE -THE POWER TO COMMUNICATE ACROSS BORDERS ALLOWS US TO ORGANIZE THE WORLD IN A DIFFERENT WAY"

"IT'S ALL ABOUT GLOBAL CITIZENSHIP. IT'S ABOUT RECOGNIZING OUR RESPONSIBILITIES TO OTHERS"

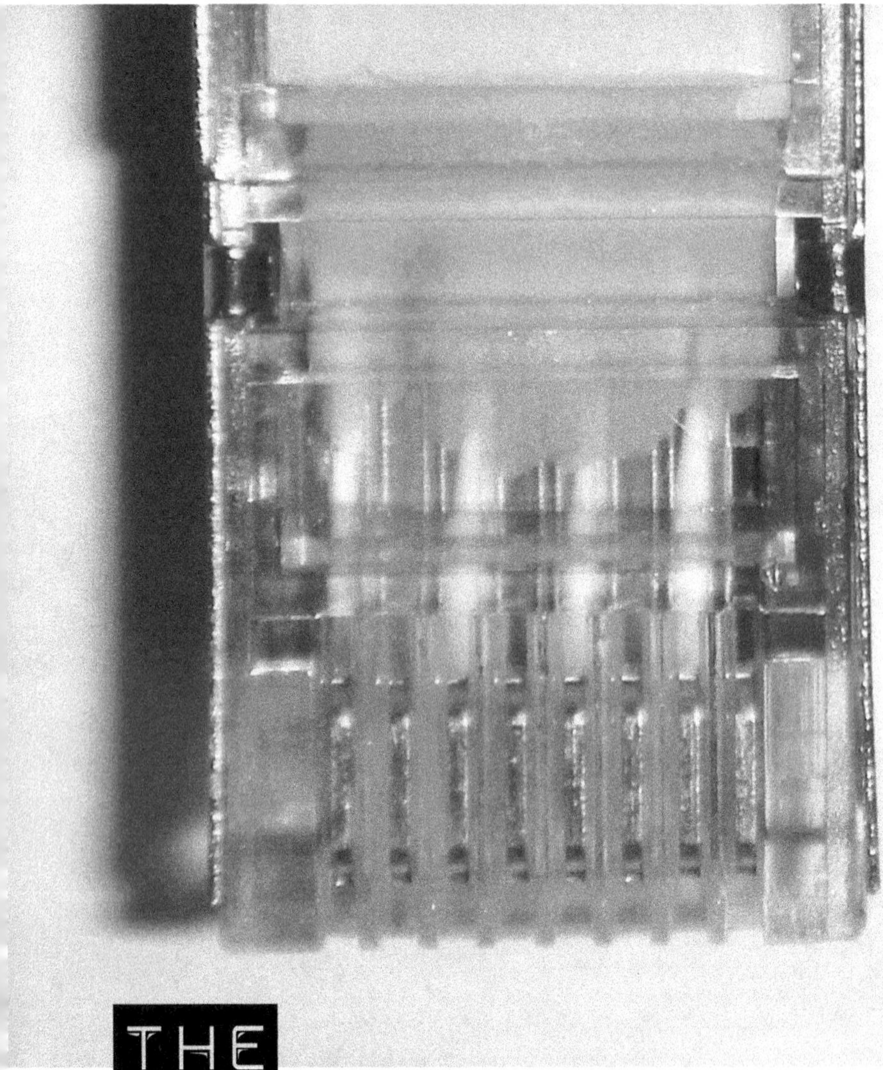

THE WORLDS LARGEST SPIDER WEB

the infrastructure of the Internet is similar to the infrastructure of utility companies making electricity or natural gas or telecommunications access available to households and enterprises. utilities provide connections of these social sites to essential resources required for carrying out social functions. access to Cyberspace has become an essential condition for social life. as such with all utilities, the essential nature of this access requires that the providers be regulated to guarantee that such access is not denied or restricted.

unbounded non-markets

Cyberspace has opened up the possibility for real time social interactions that are radically different from anything previously experienced. These interactions are less constrained by physical limitations than has been the case in the past. Indeed, by taking on alternative identities, using avatars, occupying constructed spaces within Cyberspace, it has become possible for individual homo sapiens to explore completely new ways of being, as well as interacting. The social relationships of Cyberspace are not simply market relationships, therefore, and represent an expansion in human society. The attempt by corporations and other economic agents to extend market activities within the digital realm is still at an infantile stage. The full realization of the possibilities for economic relationships within Cyberspace may be a long way in the future. The ability to adapt economic transactions to the potentials of this new space is intricately linked to expanding non-market social relationships within this same space and then adapting economic activities to this new social environment.

Markets are simply sites where humans or superorganic collections of humans (e.g. firms) engage in exchanges with one another. For most of human history, it has been necessary for bounded physical locations to serve as these sites. However, the bounded physical nature of markets has been gradually undergoing transformation and moving from the bounded physical realm into the unbounded digital realm. We saw this with the growth of digital markets for trading shares of equity in publicly traded firms over the National Association of Securities Dealers' Automated Quotation System, also called NASDAQ, which has become a major competitor with bounded physical markets for trading such shares, such as the New York Stock Exchange. At present a gap exists between the potentiality in cyberspace and the legal expressions of something in decay, a regime of rights linked to a world where boundaries were strictly enforced and ownership was the fundamental basis for exclusion and exclusivity, where the most foresighted entrepreneurs were often forced into garages and basements. Today collaboration, invention, and innovation are open source projects in a space that is boundless. The limits of the past (which continues to hold fast to the present) and the possibilities of the future (which is now) clash. What will we do? Cling to the dead or embrace the living?

today, Amazon.com has become a dominant player in the selling of books, forcing traditional bounded physical booksellers, like Barnes & Noble, to also locate in cyberspace and creating a tantalizing target for other large scale corporate players, like Apple Computer (whose presence in the marketing and sale of digital works via the iPod and successor devices pose a potential challenge to Amazon's Kindle and other ebook readers, as well as the brick and mortar booksellers). this is only the beginning of the transition from the bounded physical markets of yesterday to the unbounded markets of tomorrow, where we will be able to move relatively effortlessly from market to market, exploring a wide range of exchange possibilities and maximizing our economic autonomy. geography is becoming less and less a constraint on all economic and social relationships and the dramatic lowering of cost for production and distribution opens the door to much wider scale access to knowledge than has heretofore been known. This is the second Guttenberg-like revolution in knowledge diffusion.

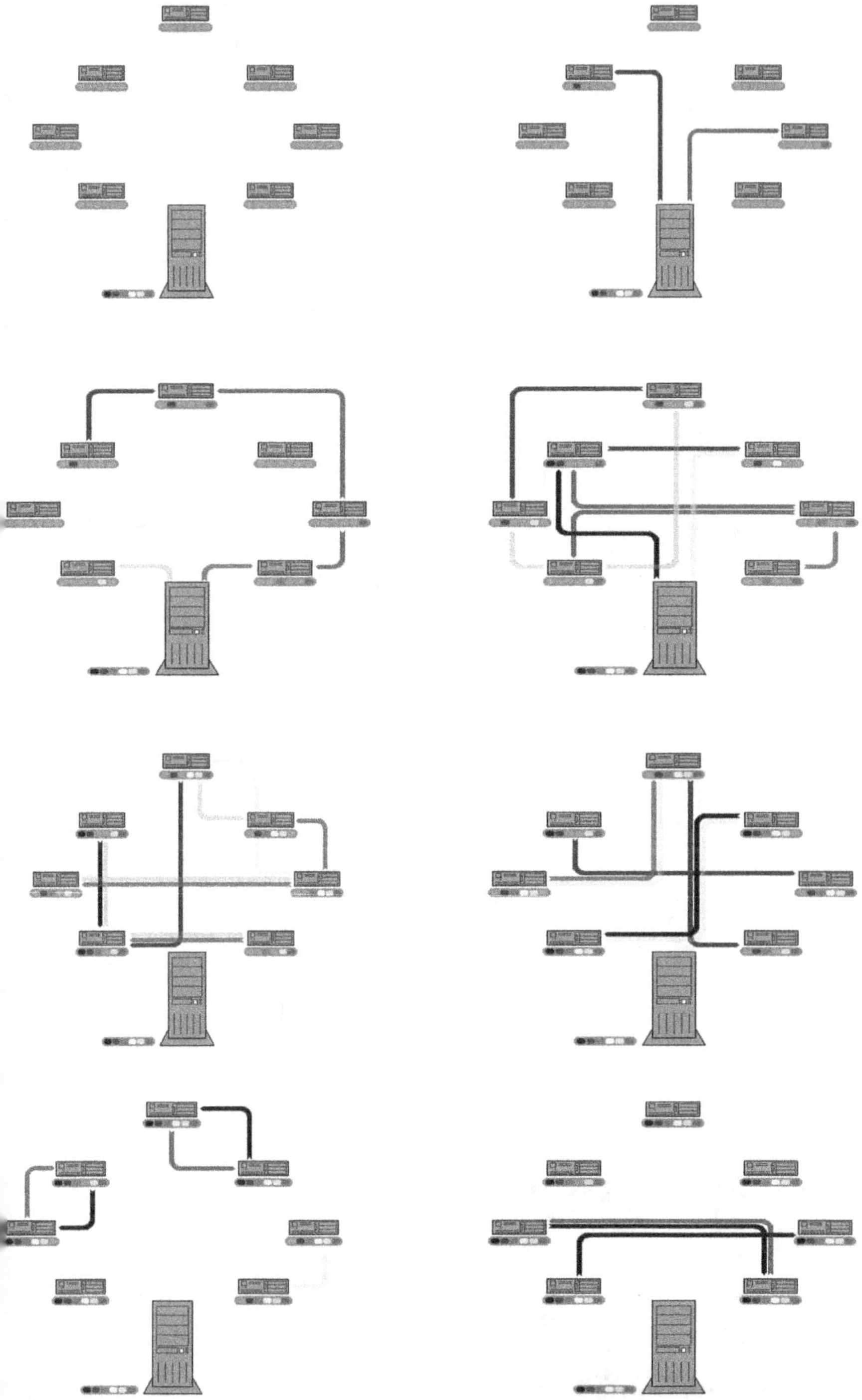

12

Technomasses

Human social formations have always been driven, in part, by revolutions in technological gestalts: the agricultural revolution, the commercial revolution, and the industrial revolution are cases in point.

Knowledge is the basis for invention and innovation. Invention and innovation allows for the expansion of human potential. Knowledge is therefore the substance of all economic development and economic growth is only sustainable with economic development. Today, knowledge is increasingly embodied in digital forms. Knowledge diffusion has become relatively easy to accomplish and the speed of such diffusion is increasing exponentially. The potential for human culture evolution has never been greater and is expanding every moment at an accelerating rate.

This is the age of the decentralized Technomass.

—Welcome.

“The new electronic interdependence recreates the world in the image of a global village”

—Marshall McLuhan

Marshall McLuhan, 60’s
philosopher and scholar
master of media theory.

we began.

:0)

All human beings are born free and equal

Universal Declarations of Human Rights Ω Adopted by the United Nations General Assembly on December 10, 1948 at the Palais de Chaillot in Paris. Ω The "Most Translated Document" in the world. Ω In 1966 the General Assembly adopted the two detailed Covenants, which complete the International Bill of Human Rights. Ω (2009, May 28) In Wikipedia, the free encyclopedia. Retrieved May 30, 2009, from *http://en.wikipedia.org/wiki/Universal_Declaration_of_Human_Rights* **(CC)**

"the empire

Winston Churchill Ω British politician. Ω Was Prime Minister of the United Kingdom from 1940 to 1945. Ω Speech at Harvard University, September 6, 1943, in The Oxford Dictionary of Quotations (1999), Knowles & Partington, Oxford University Press, p. 215. Ω (2009, December 5) In Wikiquotes. Retrieved May 25, 2009, from *http://en.wikiquote.org/wiki/Winston_Churchill* **(CC)**

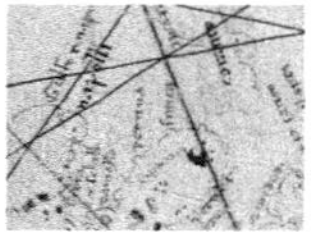

Cartographic Artifact Ω Oldest original cartographic artifact in the Library of Congress: a nautical chart of the Mediterranean Sea - second quarter of the fourteenth century. Ω Library of Congress, (2009, October 20) In Wikiquotes. Retrieved November 18, 2009, from *http://en.wikipedia.org/wiki/File:Mediterranean_chart_fourteenth_century2.jpg* **(PD)**

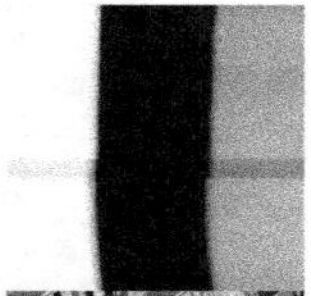

Video Signal by Txo Ω Image of video signal line 18 Ω The origins of mechanical television can be traced back to the discovery of the photoconductivity of the element selenium by Willoughby Smith in 1873 Ω (2009, July 29) In Wikimedia Commons. Retrieved November 18, 2009, from *http://commons.wikimedia.org/wiki/File:18_P.jpg* **(PD)**

Flags of the World Ω Brockhaus and Efron Encyclopedic Dictionary (1890—1907) Ω Image created between 1890 and 1907 Ω (2009, December 2) In Wikimedia Commons. Retrieved December 8, 2009, from *http://commons.wikimedia.org/wiki/File:Brockhaus_and_Efron_Encyclopedic_Dictionary_b71_098-2.jpg* **(PD)**

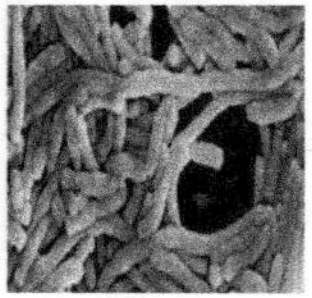

Salmonella Ω Salmonella are closely related to the Escherichia genus and are found worldwide in warm- and cold-blooded animals, in humans, and in nonliving habitats. Ω (2009, September 27) In Wikimedia Commons. Retrieved October 5, 2009, from *http://commons.wikimedia.org/wiki/File:Pseudomonas.jpg* **(PD)**

Acheulean Ω Given to an archaeological industry of stone tool manufacture associated with prehistoric hominins during the Lower Palaeolithic era across Africa and much of West Asia and Europe. Ω (2006, January 6) In Wikipedia, the free encyclopedia. Retrieved October 5, 2009, from *http://en.wikipedia.org/wiki/File:Acheuleanhandaxes.jpg* **(PD)**

Karl Marx Ω British politician. Ω German political philosopher, political economist, and social theorist. Ω (2009, December 8) In Wikiquotes. Retrieved Dicember 2, 2009, from *http://en.wikiquote.org/wiki/Karl_Marx* **(CC)**

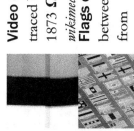

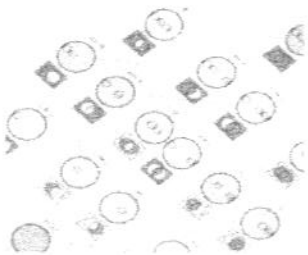

Hasse diagram (modified) **Ω** Simple picture of a finite partially ordered set, forming a drawing of the transitive reduction of the partial order. **Ω** (2009, August 24) In Wikipedia, the free encyclopedia. Retrieved October 12, 2009, from *http://en.wikipedia.org/wiki/File:Logical_connectives_Hasse_diagram.svg* **(CC)**

USA Night **Ω** United States of America **Ω** Satellite image showing the light output at night in the United States **Ω** (2004, September 21) In Wikimedia Commons. Retrieved November 12, 2009, from *http://commons.wikimedia.org/wiki/File:Usa_night.gif* **(PD)**

CERN Server Room by Florian Hirzinger **Ω** European Organization for Nuclear Research. **Ω** The World Wide Web began as a CERN project called ENQUIRE, initiated by Tim Berners-Lee in 1989 and Robert Cailliau in 1990. **Ω** (2009, March 12) In Wikimedia Commons. Retrieved May 23, 2009, from *http://commons.wikimedia.org/wiki/File:CERN_Server_03.jpg* **(CC)**

Servers at LAAS by Guillaume Paumier **Ω** Laboratoire d'analyse et d'architecture des systèmes. **Ω** (2007, November 11) In Wikipedia, the free encyclopedia. Retrieved October 4, 2009, from *http://commons.wikimedia.org/wiki/File:Servers_at_LAAS_%28FDLS_2007%29_0389.jpg* **(CC)**

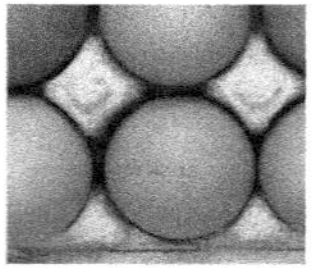

Eggs with coding in Netherlands by Eicode Nederland **Ω** Bround or oval cell laid by the female of any number of different species, consisting of an ovum surrounded by layers of membranes and an outer casing. **Ω** (2006, August 17) In Wikiquotes. Retrieved Dicember 3, 2009, from *http://commons.wikimedia.org/wiki/File:Eicode_Nederland.jpg* **(CC)**

Woods in Hampshire College by José Fuentes **Ω** Hampshire College has no grades, no majors, no exams. **Ω** (2009) Jose Fuentes **(CC)**

New York Stock Exchange by Jose Fuentes (modified) **Ω** Slocated at 11 Wall Street in lower Manhattan, New York City, New York, USA. It is the largest stock exchange in the world by United States dollar value of its listed companies' securities.. **Ω** (2009, October 22) Jose Fuentes **(CC)**

President Andrew Jackson **Ω** 7th President of the United States (1829–1837) **Ω** Protector of popular democracy and individual liberty, checkered by his support for Indian removal and slavery. **Ω** (2008, November 6) In Wikimedia Commons. Retrieved November 22, 2009, from *http://en.wikipedia.org/wiki/File:Andrew_Jackson.jpg* **(PD)**

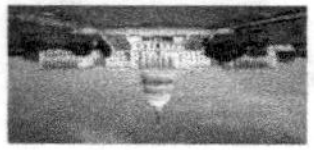

United States Capitol by Architect of the Capitol **Ω** Meeting place of the United States Congress. **Ω** Located in Washington, D.C. **Ω** (2009, August 11) In Wikimedia Commons. Retrieved December 8, 2009, from *http://en.wikipedia.org/wiki/File:United_States_Capitol_-_west_front.jpg* **(PD)**

ATM (modified) **Ω** HK Sheung Wan Jervois Street Shanghai Commercial Bank ATM **Ω** (2008, August 18) In Wikimedia Commons. Retrieved October 7, 2009, from *http://commons.wikimedia.org/wiki/File:HK_Sheung_Wan_Jervois_Street_Shanghai_Commercial_Bank_ATM.JPG* **(CC)**

US 20 Dollar Bill **Ω** Denomination of United States currency. U.S. President Andrew Jackson is currently featured on the front side of the bill, which is why the twenty-dollar bill is often called a "Jackson," while the White House is featured on the reverse side. **Ω** (2008, March 14) In Wikipedia, the free encyclopedia. Retrieved November 15, 2009, from *http://commons.wikimedia.org/wiki/File:US_$20_1985_Note_Front.jpg* **(PD)**

Bank of America by Brian Katt Ω Founded and originally headquartered in San Francisco, California [5], is now headquartered in Charlotte, North Carolina. **Ω** (2008, March 14) In Wikiquotes. Retrieved October 26, 2009, from *http://commons.wikimedia.org/wiki/File:Bank_highlander.jpg* **(CC)**

Hasse diagram Ω Act to provide authority for the Federal Government to purchase and insure certain types of troubled assets for the purposes of providing stability to and preventing disruption in the economy and financial system. **Ω** US Government Printing Office. Retrieved December 11, 2009, from *http://www.gpo.gov/fdsys/pkg/PLAW-110publ343/content-detail.html*

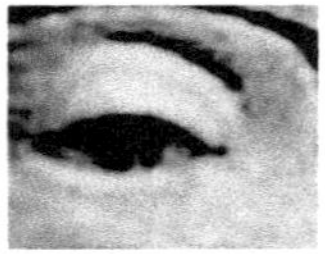

Alan Greenspan Ω American economist. **Ω** Chairman of the Federal Reserve of the United States from 1987 to 2006. **Ω** (2005, February 19) In Wikimedia Commons. Retrieved November 12, 2009, from *http://commons.wikimedia.org/wiki/File:Mvc-017x.jpg* **(PD)**

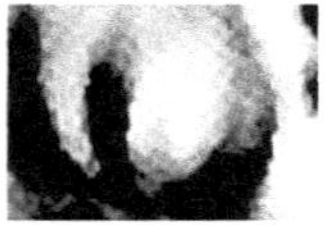

Uncle Sam Ω National personification of the United States **Ω** Usage of the term dating from the War of 1812. **Ω** (2005, September 27) In Wikimedia Commons. Retrieved October 12, 2009, from *http://commons.wikimedia.org/wiki/File:Uncle_Sam_%28pointing_finger%29.jpg* **(PD)**

Bad-War Ω Swiss and Landsknecht soldiers engage in the exceptionally-fierce hand to hand combat known as "bad war." **Ω** (2006, August 29) In Wikipedia, the free encyclopedia. Retrieved October 6, 2009, from *http://commons.wikimedia.org/wiki/File:Bad-war.jpg* **(PD)**

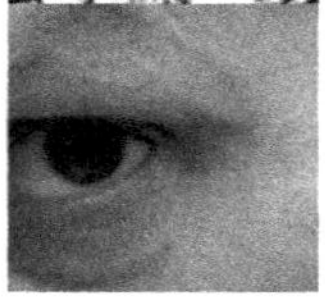

Treasury Secretary Timothy Geithner and NEC Director Larry Summers by Official White House Photo by Pete Souza Ω Meeting with President Barack Obama in the Oval Office 2/11/09. **Ω** (2006, August 17) From Flickr, Retrieved Dicember 16, 2009, from *http://www.flickr.com/photos/whitehouse/3484824164/* **(PD)**

Obama Health Care Speech to Joint Session of Congress by Lawrence Jackson Ω President Barack Obama speaks to a joint session of Congress regarding health care reform. **Ω** (2009, September 24) In Wikimedia Commons. Retrieved November 4, 2009, from *http://en.wikipedia.org/wiki/File:Obama_Health_Care_Speech_to_Joint_Session_of_Congress.jpg* **(PD)**

Jesus Christus Ω Central figure of Christianity, which views him as the Messiah foretold in the Old Testament. **Ω** (2008, January 22) In Wikimedia Commons. Retrieved November 15, 2009, from *http://commons.wikimedia.org/wiki/File:Jesus_Sinai_Icon.jpg* **(PD)**

Smith Premier Ω This image was first published in the 1st (1876–1899), 2nd (1904–1926) or 3rd (1923–1937) edition of Nordisk Familjebok. **Ω** (2005, December 6) In Wikimedia Commons. Retrieved November 28, 2009, from *http://commons.wikimedia.org/wiki/File:Skrifmaskin,_Smith_Premier-maskin,_Nordisk_familjebok.png* **(PD)**

Young Woman and Broken Window by LennieZ Ω In Wikimedia Commons, Retrieved Dicember 15, 2009, from http://commons.wikimedia.org/wiki/File:Young_woman_and_broken_window-2.jpg **(CC)**

Liberty Leading the People. Ω Painting by Eugène Delacroix commemorating the July Revolution of 1830, which toppled Charles X. **Ω** A woman personifying Liberty leads the people forward over the bodies of the fallen, holding the tricolore flag of the French Revolution . **Ω** (2009, July 21) In Wikimedia Commons. Retrieved November 12, 2009, from *http://en.wikipedia.org/wiki/File:Eug%C3%A8ne_Delacroix_-_La_libert%C3%A9_guidant_le_peuple.jpg* **(PD)**

YOU SHOULD THINK OF FREE AS IN NOT AS IN FREE BEER

The Free Software Definition by Free Software Foundation Ω A non-profit corporation founded by Richard Stallman on 4 October 1985 to support the free software movement, a copyleft-based movement which aims to promote the universal freedom to distribute and modify computer software. Ω From GNU Operating System and Free Software Foundation website. Retrieved December 14, 2009, from *http://www.gnu.org/philosophy/free-sw.html*

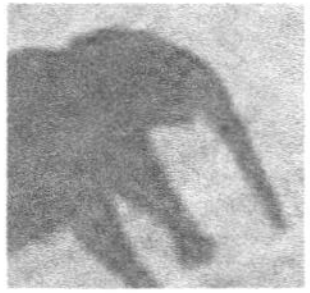

Hunters and Elephant, Ω San Bushmen Rock Art near Stadsaal Cave in the Cederberg. Cederberg mountains and nature reserve are located near Clanwilliam, approximately 300 km north of Cape Town, South Africa. Ω (2008, May 19) In Wikimedia Commons. Retrieved November 26, 2009, from *http://en.wikipedia.org/wiki/File:San_Rock_Art_-_Cederberg.jpg* **(CC)**

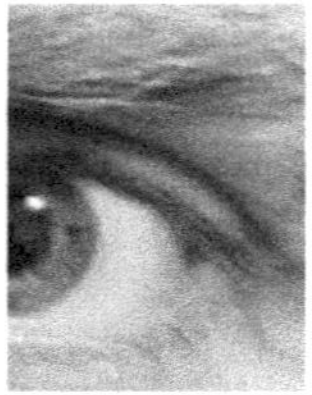

Benjamin Mako Hill by Mika Matsuzaki Ω Debian hacker, intellectual property researcher, activist and author. Ω Senior Researcher at the MIT Sloan School of Management where he studies free software communities and business models. Ω Graduate of Hampshire College Ω Usage of the term dating from the War of 1812. Ω (2008, August 7) In Wikimedia Commons. Retrieved October 11, 2009, from *http://en.wikipedia.org/wiki/File:Benji.jpg* **(CC)**

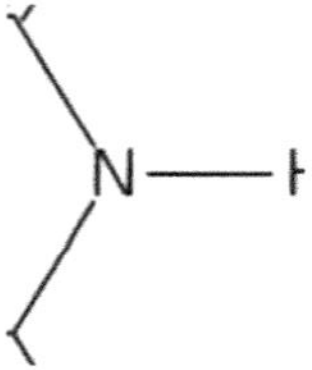

GC DNA Base Pair by Isilanes Ω GC base pair demonstrating three intermolecular hydrogen bonds. Ω DNA with high GC-content is more stable than DNA with low GC-content, but contrary to popular belief, the hydrogen bonds do not stabilize the DNA significantly and stabilization is mainly due to stacking interactions.. Ω (2007, June 12) In Wikipedia, the free encyclopedia. Retrieved October 1, 2009, from *http://en.wikipedia.org/wiki/File:GC_DNA_base_pair.svg* **(PD)**

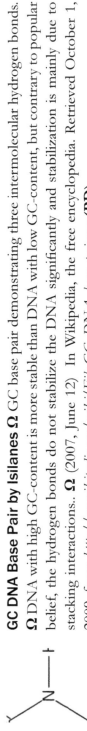

GNU Ω Computer operating system composed entirely of free software. **Ω** Its name is a recursive acronym for "GNU's not Unix!". **Ω** (2009, November 22) In Wikimedia Commons. Retrieved November 22, 2009, from *http://en.wikipedia.org/wiki/File:Heckert_GNU_white.svg* **(Free Art License)**

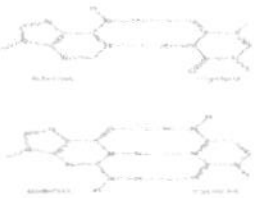

AT DNA Base Pair by Isilanes Ω An AT base pair demonstrating two intermolecular hydrogen bonds. **Ω** (2007, June 12) In Wikipedia, the free encyclopedia. Retrieved October 1, 2009, from *http://en.wikipedia.org/wiki/File:AT_DNA_base_pair.svg/* **(PD)**

Indian Elephant Zuze by 663highland Ω Indian Elephant Zuze in the Kobe Oji Zoo, Kobe, Japan. **Ω** Large land mammals in two genera of the family Elephantidae: Elephas and Loxodonta. **Ω** (2006, March 12) In Wikimedia Commons. Retrieved November 4, 2009, from *http://commons.wikimedia.org/wiki/File:Elephas_maximus_bengalensis02_1920.jpg* **(CC)**

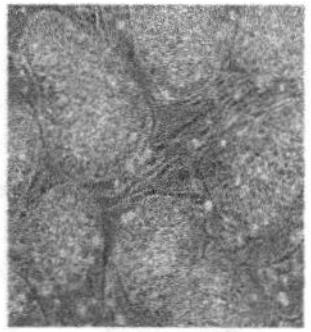

Human Embryonic Stem Cells by Nissim Benvenisty Ω Found in most, if not all, multi-cellular organisms. **Ω** They are characterized by the ability to renew themselves through mitotic cell division and differentiating into a diverse range of specialized cell types.. **Ω** (2006, December 4) In Wikimedia Commons. Retrieved November 8, 2009, from *http://en.wikipedia.org/wiki/File:Human_embryonic_stem_cells.png* **(CC)**

The First Earthrise Photographed by Humans; by Frank Borman Ω Picture taken on December 24, 1968 **Ω** Apollo 8 was the first human spaceflight mission to achieve a velocity sufficient to allow escape from the gravitational field of planet Earth; the first to be captured by and escape from the gravitational field of another celestial body. **Ω** (2007, December 28) In Wikimedia Commons, Retrieved Dicember 15, 2009, from http://en.wikipedia.org/wiki/File:AS8-13-2329.jpg **(PD)**

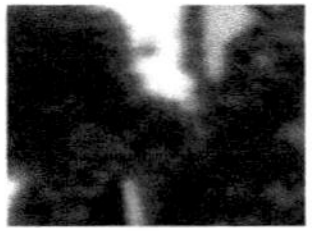

Jackson Pollock: Number 31 Ω Oil and enamel paint on canvas, 8' 10" x 17' 5 5/8" (269.5 x 530.8 cm). Sidney and Harriet Janis Collection Fund. **Ω** Photograph by Scalleja, In Flickr. Retrieved November 12, 2009, from *http://www.flickr.com/photos/scalleja/578311231/* **(CC)**

Jackson Pollock Ω Paul Jackson Pollock (1912-01-28 — 1956-08-11) was one of the leading artists and an influential American painter in the Abstract Expressionist movement, together with Willem de Kooning. **Ω** interview by William Wright, Summer 1950 (for broadcasting, but never used); as quoted in Abstract Expressionism: Creators and Critics, ed. Clifford Ross, Abrahams Publishers, New York 1990, pp. 139-140. **Ω** In Wikiquotes. Retrieved December 11, 2009, from *http://en.wikiquote.org/wiki/Jackson_Pollockl* **(CC)**

The Caterpillar by Sir John Tenniel Ω You know a Caterpillar has got quantities of legs: you can see more of them, further down." (Carroll, Lewis. The Nursery "Alice". Dover Publications (1966), p27). **Ω** (2006, May 22) In Wikimedia Commons. Retrieved November 27, 2009, from *http://commons.wikimedia.org/wiki/File:Alice_05a-1116x1492.jpg* **(PD)**

US-Mexico Border by Jesse Allen Ω DNASA image created by Jesse Allen, using data provided courtesy of NASA/GSFC/METI/ERSDAC/JAROS, and U.S./Japan ASTER Science Team. **Ω** (2009, April 12) In Wikimedia Commons. Retrieved October 11, 2009, from *hhttp://en.wikipedia.org/wiki/File:El_Paso,_Texas.jpg* **(CC)**

Tijuana and San Diego Border by James Reyes Ω The beach on the Pacific Ocean at the U.S.-Mexico border from the Mexican side. **Ω** (2008, May 17) In Wikipedia, the free encyclopedia. Retrieved October 19, 2009, from *http://en.wikipedia.org/wiki/File:Borderbeachtj.jpg* **(PD)**

School Bus Ω Houston, TX., 9/8/2005 -- Louisianna Elementary school students wave good bye to their parents from their school bus as they leave the Reliant center for their first day of school in Texas. They are sheltered at the Reliant center and were evacuated from Louisianna when New Orleans was evacuated. FEMA photo/Andrea Booher. **Ω** (2009, October 15) In Wikipedia, the free encyclopedia. Retrieved October 22, 2009, from *http://commons.wikimedia.org/wiki/File:FEMA_-_15118_-_Photograph_by_Andrea_Booher_taken_on_09-08-2005_in_Texas.jpg* **(PD)**

Class of 2007, USAF Academy Graduation Hat Hurray Toss by Beverly & Pack's Ω U.S. Air Force Academy graduates throw their hats in the air as the Thunderbirds fly overhead signaling the end of the Air Force Academy graduation ceremony, Colorado Springs, Colo., May 30, 2007. **Ω** From Flickr. Retrieved November 11, 2009, from *http://www.flickr.com/photos/walkadog/3573598435* **(CC)**

Main Reading Room, Library of Congress (Jefferson Building), Washington, D.C. by Andreas Praefcke Ω Research library of the United States Congress and is the oldest federal cultural institution in the United States. **Ω** Located in three buildings in Washington, D.C., it is the largest library in the world by shelf space and holds the largest number of books.. **Ω** (2007,June 20) In Wikimedia Commons. Retrieved November 8, 2009, from *http://commons.wikimedia.org/wiki/File:LoC_Main_Reading_Room.jpg* **(CC)**

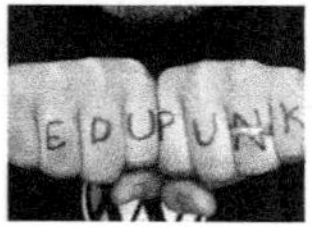

Jim Groom as Edupunk by umwdtlt Ω An approach to teaching and learning practices that result from a do it yourself (DIY) attitude. **Ω** (2008, June 6) In Wikimedia Commons, Retrieved Dicember 19, 2009, from *http://en.*wikipedia.org/wiki/File:Edupunk.jpg **(CC)**

How to Make Your Own Television Receiver Ω Experimenter Publishing's WRNY began transmitting experimental television in August 1928 to viewers in New York City. Most viewers built their own set. **Ω** (2008, August 6) In Wikimedia Commons,Retrieved November 12, 2009, from *http://commons.wikimedia.org/wiki/File:Radio_News_Nov_1928_pg422.png* **(PD)**

Passport Stamps from Qatar, UAE, French Polynesia, Spain and the US Ω Document, issued by a national government, which certifies, for the purpose of international travel, the identity and nationality of its holder. **Ω** (2008, June 24) In Wikimedia Commons, Retrieved December 11, 2009, from *http://commons.wikimedia.org/wiki/File:Passport_pages_30-31.jpg* **(CC)**

Partial Map of the Internet Ω Based on the January 15, 2005 data found on opte.org. Each line is drawn between two nodes, representing two IP addresses. **Ω** The length of the lines are indicative of the delay between those two nodes. **Ω** (2007, January 7) In Wikimedia Commons, Retrieved December 11, 2009, from *http://en.wikipedia.org/wiki/File:Internet_map_1024.jpg* **(CC)**

U.K. Chancellor of the Exchequer Gordon Brown at the Commonwealth Finance Ministers Press Conference by IMF Ω Prime Minister of the United Kindom **Ω** (2007, July 3) In Wikimedia Commons. Retrieved November 1, 2009, from *http://commons.wikimedia.org/wiki/File:GordonBrown2004.JPGpg* **(PD)**

Ethernet Cable Ω Category 5 cable is a twisted pair high signal integrity cable type often referred to as Cat5. **Ω** (2005, December 27) In Wikimedia Commons. Retrieved October 12, 2009, from *http://commons.wikimedia.org/wiki/File:Vergleich_2von2_Crossoverkabel.gif* **(PD)**

Servers at LAAS-CNRS in Toulouse, France by Guillaume Paumier Ω (2007, November 11) In Wikipedia, the free encyclopedia. Retrieved October 19, 2009, from *http://commons.wikimedia.org/wiki/File:Servers_at_LAAS_%28FDLS_2007%29_0390.jpg* **(CC)**

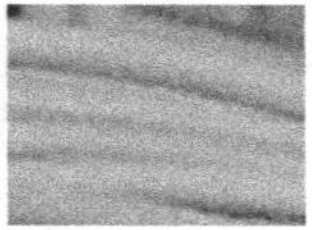

Optical Fiver Ω Qlogic SANbox 5600 switch with optical FC connectors installed. Test lab of BiTech company (Moscow, Russia). **Ω** (2009, February 7) In Wikipedia, the free encyclopedia. Retrieved October 22, 2009, from *http://commons.wikimedia.org/wiki/File:ML-QLOGICNFCCONN.JPG* **(PD)**

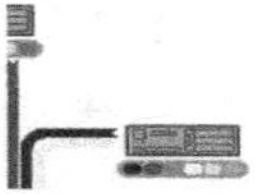

Bitorrent Protocol Ω This animated gif ilustrates the bitorrent protocol for sharing files. **Ω** (2005, April 5) In Wikimedia Commons. Retrieved November 9, 2009, from *http://en.wikipedia.org/wiki/File:Torrentcomp_small.gif* **(CC)**

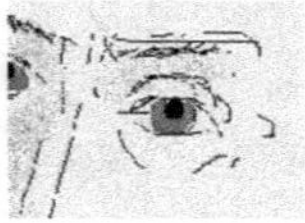

Marshall McLuhan Ω Canadian educator, philosopher, and scholar. **Ω** (2006, September 6) In Wikimedia Commons, Retrieved Dicember 19, 2009, from *http://commons.wikimedia.org/wiki/File:Herbert_Marshall_McLuhan_drawing.jpg* **(CC)**

Fast Movement by jonasj Ω From Flickr, Retrieved November 12, 2009, from *http://www.flickr.com/photos/jonasj/344362310/* **(CC)**

Jose Fuentes is a research fellow in computer science at Carnegie Mellon and graduate of Hampshire College with a concentration in psychology and economics

Satyananda Gabriel is a professor of economics and finance and chair of the economics department at Mount Holyoke College in South Hadley, Massachusetts.

RISING TECHNOMASS

THE POLITICAL ECONOMY OF SOCIAL TRANSFORMATION IN CYBERSPACE

Jose Fuentes
Satyananda Gabriel

www.ingramcontent.com/pod-product-compliance
Lightning Source LLC
LaVergne TN
LVHW022310060326
832902LV00020B/3386
* 9 7 8 1 9 3 5 3 2 3 0 2 0 *